Celebrate a...
Country Woman Christmas

It's that magical time of year! Choirs sing and church bells ring…trees sparkle with tinsel and lights…and stockings are hung by the chimney in joyful anticipation.

There's nothing quite like Christmas, with its bounty of cheer and goodwill—and there's nothing quite like the way it's celebrated in the *country* either.

So, with that in mind, we've again rounded up some very merry sights, sounds, aromas, flavors and memories of the season—straight from the homes of readers just like you—and bound them into this second annual edition in our one-of-a-kind *Country Woman Christmas* keepsake book series.

Jolly Goodies. From appetizers to desserts, you now have 90-some never-before-published food favorites of families across the country to add to your mainstay of holiday recipes. Each can be made with ingredients you likely already have on hand, and each is as *delicious* as it is convenient—we made sure of that by testing it ourselves in our *Country Woman* kitchen.

So, whether you're having a bunch of folks over to munch brunch…or a family sit-down dinner with all the trimmings,

you'll find just what you need to make this Christmas even more memorable.

Merry Makings. You have dozens of inventively original Christmas craft projects to choose from, too—complete with simple-to-follow instructions, patterns, charts, etc. right alongside. Plus, knowing how hectic the holiday season can get at our houses, we've made sure most are quick-and-easy! They're perfect for gift-giving *or* for decking your halls.

Looking for decorating ideas? Take a "sneak peek" into the homes of the other country women featured here and see how they've added personal homemade touches to the holidays.

You'll also meet some rural women whose talents really "shine" this time of year…as well as treat yourself (and your family) to touching fiction and poetry, beautiful photos, nostalgic remembrances of Christmases past and much more.

More in Store! With a colorful new edition being added to this series every year, you can look forward to many more country-flavored holiday celebrations. But, for now, simply settle back with *Country Woman Christmas 1997*. We hope you enjoy it as much as we've enjoyed bringing it to you!

3

Senior Editor
Kathy Pohl

Food Editors
Mary Beth Jung
Coleen Martin

Associate Food Editor
Sue A. Jurack

Assistant Food Editor
Corinne Willkomm

Senior Home Economist
Mary Fullmer

**Test Kitchen
Home Economist**
Karla Spies

Test Kitchen Assistants
Judith Scholovich
Sherry Smalley
Suzi Hampton

Craft Editors
Tricia Coogan
Jane Craig

Associate Editors
Kathleen Zimmer
Sharon Selz
Faithann Stoner
Kristine Krueger

Editorial Assistant
Heather Kuenzi

Art Director
Gail Engeldahl

Assistant Art Director
Julie Wagner

Cover Designer
Vicky Marie Moseley

Illustrator
Linda Dzik

Photographers
Scott Anderson
Glenn Thiesenhusen

Food Photography Artist
Stephanie Marchese

Photo Studio Coordinator
Anne Schimmel

Production Assistant
Claudia Wardius

© 1997 Reiman Publications, L.P.
5400 S. 60th Street
Greendale WI 53129

International Standard Book
Number: 0-89821-211-1
International Standard Serial
Number: 1093-6750

INSIDE...

AND MUCH MORE!

Photo Contributors: p. 7—Dale Riggs; pp. 8-10—Fred Rollison; p. 49—Doug Cripe/Doug's Studio; pp. 50-51—Iris Riley; p. 68—Tim Bommel; p. 69—Rikshots Photography; p. 91—Douglas Reichert; p. 93—Carmen Tritten; p. 110—The Guilded Angel Photos by Debbie.

Christmastime

Come, let's light the Christmas candles,
Hang a wreath upon the door,
Decorate the tree in splendor…
For it's Christmastime once more.

Come, let's bake the Christmas cookies,
Make the fruitcake as before,
Put a bow on every package…
For it's Christmastime once more.

Come, let's welcome in the season,
Sing the carols we adore,
Worship at the church with gladness…
For it's Christmastime once more.

—Beverly J. Anderson
Ft. Lauderdale, Florida

BRIGHT IDEAS in Martins' illuminating display include lighthearted 58-foot snowman (above).

Couple's Christmas Project Lights up Lives for Others

WHEN Christmas arrives around Great Bend, Kansas, Carol Martin gets busy sparking the spirit of the season…in tens of thousands of hearts.

"Our Christmas Fantasy Village is a 4-1/2-acre display of what this time of year is all about," Carol explains from the hobby farm-turned-wonderland she and husband Bob run. "We look at it as a gift to share with others."

Back when the spectacle was unwrapped, 20 years ago, it featured a power pole dressed up like a Christmas tree with six simple strands of lights. Each season has found the couple adding more radiant decorations until, today, some 100,000 people annually witness the tradition.

"Here to greet them is a 58-foot snowman, animated holiday characters and a teddy bear carousel," Carol relates. "The Candyland Express—a small-scale train—provides rides. After having their picture taken in an antique sleigh, families can warm up by the wood stove with cocoa and cider.

"Recent additions are a church, a Nativity scene and a stable with live animals for petting. Above, the star of Bethlehem illuminates the scene."

Plenty of pulling together makes it all possible. Family (including the Martins' four grown children and seven grandkids) and friends by the dozens pitch in for the *600 hours* of preparation required. Bob, the owner of a power line construction business, oversees the countless bulbs and over 1 mile of underground wire that gets everything ready to glow. (A $1-a-person admission lightens the electric bill.)

"There's Christmas cheer, too, in our Fantasy Country Gift Shop," Carol states of the 30 fully decorated trees, crafts she makes, ornaments and more. "Bob even exhibits his holiday antiques —tree stands, cards and candy tins."

And, come Christmas Eve, the Martins pause and collect *their* gifts—comments like that of the wide-eyed youngster who once piped up, "So *this* is where Santa Claus lives!"

Editor's Note: *Christmas Fantasy Village is open Sunday-Thursday 6:30-9:30 p.m. and Friday-Saturday 6:30-10:30 p.m. Thanksgiving Day through Christmas Day. It's located 3 miles south of 10th and Main Streets in Great Bend on Highway 281. For details, contact Carol Martin, Rt. 2, Box 78, Great Bend KS 67530; 1-316/792-8805.* ❁

WATTS GOING ON at their merry prairie farm makes the holidays sparkle for Carol and Bob (in sleigh above). Double vision of Yule's light side is provided by reflecting pool to 100,000 visitors.

WELCOME TO MY COUNTRY KITCHEN

By Mary Frances Hanson of Seneca, South Carolina

SPRUCING UP kitchen, Mary Frances Hanson has Christmas branching from tiny tree at sinkside, evergreens on plates, table where she, husband Robert share merry moments (above) to green window valances.

MY KITCHEN takes on a special country glow during the holidays...naturally! Decorating with rich red poinsettias and evergreen accents is my way of bringing the great outdoors *inside* to enjoy.

The look fits right in with our woodsy surroundings, here on the shore of Lake Keowee. At Christmastime, I accentuate the cozy warmth of my kitchen's wall-to-wall woodwork with cardinal red and pine green flourishes. Next to the sink, I set a small spruce. Then I hang a swag of poinsettia garland on the wall.

But that's merely the beginning of my merry kitchen makeover. With food such an important part of the season, I pack away my everyday dishes and replace them with plates featuring a perky pine design.

When special company comes, I love to set a gala table. The same pretty pines that are on my dishes circle the white tablecloth, and an evergreen centerpiece trimmed with gold makes a conversation piece in itself.

Merry Mornings

Even when it's just my husband, Robert, and me, we start our days in a holiday way, drinking our morning coffee from Christmas mugs I store on a mug "tree" on the counter.

Speaking of the kitchen counter, I could devote lots of space here to the space it gives *me*. It runs the length of one wall and curves around to two other walls. That allows me all the room I need for both cooking and decorating!

At Christmas, I can display my holiday tea and coffee service in a corner and still have surface to spare to whip up one of my holiday coffee cakes. The extra space comes in especially handy, though, when I prepare a holiday meal for our big family of five children, their spouses and 11 grandchildren.

With the little ones here, I keep fresh-baked treats in my Santa cookie jar. (I always wonder if that jolly old fellow wears such a big smile because of all the snitchin' stories he could tell!)

My kitchen island is another place for my festive flourishes. I set up my figurines of Santa and Mrs. Claus on a pretty green table runner. Santa's warming himself at the stove, while Mrs. Claus fixes dinner.

Hearty Taste of Heritage

I'm as busy as Mrs. Claus in my Christmas kitchen, making my family's traditional holiday favorites. First, I take the Swedish waffle iron from the soffit—it's on display next to the plates and teapots I collect—and mix a batch of pizzelles, the kind of cookies Robert's Scandinavian mother used to make.

After we return from church on Christmas Eve, I usually pay tribute to my Italian heritage by cooking a traditional meal of fish and pasta. Once we've opened presents Christmas morning, I'm back to Scandinavian style preparing another of Robert's requests—Swedish pancakes.

With all that cooking, there's plenty of cleanup. But no one protests when I ask them to help. Instead, they grow wide-eyed. The two large kitchen windows face the southeast and northwest...the view of the lake, with the Blue Ridge Mountains in the background, is spectacular.

Enhancing the scenic sights, the windows all have valances of forest green, and one picture window has a gathered ↻

fabric treatment that frames the panes.

The Christmas spirit doesn't stop at the kitchen door either. We spread it throughout the house. Our living room opens up to a lofty cathedral ceiling, which gives us the leeway to bring home a *huge* Christmas tree.

Surrounded by Spirit

Every bench or table holds Christmas treasures. I devote two shelves to my light-up ceramic village, for instance, while my collection of pewter, wood and ceramic Santas takes up a table of its own.

The little teddy bear who sits on the piano bench never fails to win a grin from the grandkids—this time of year, he sports a holiday hat of red and green.

We even dress up the kitchen deck a bit by hanging evergreen wreaths on the glass doors. When the wind flutters the red bows, Christmas is truly in the air.

Thank you for letting me share my own slice of Christmas cheer this year. As you can see, our house is seasonally spiced all over. And my Yuletide kitchen's where it all starts cookin'! ❊

YULE'S TIED into Mary Frances' work area wrapped in wooden cabinetry. Figurines of Santa, Mrs. Claus on island (inset) suggest real goodies Grandma Hanson whips up for family (below).

Holiday Brunch

CHOCOLATE MARBLE BREAD
Rosina Sacks, Copley, Pennsylvania
(Pictured below)

My mother made this bread many Sundays for breakfast—and, if I was lucky, there'd be some left to savor Monday and Tuesday mornings as well! Just a whiff of this beautiful bread baking brings back treasured memories.

   7 to 7-1/2 cups all-purpose flour
   1 package (1/4 ounce) active dry yeast
   2 cups milk
  1/2 cup sugar
  1/4 cup butter *or* margarine
   1 teaspoon salt
   2 eggs
  1/4 cup baking cocoa
GLAZE:
   1 cup confectioners' sugar
   1 tablespoon milk
  1/4 cup chopped walnuts

In a mixing bowl, combine 3 cups flour and yeast. In a saucepan, heat milk, sugar, butter and salt to 120°-130°, stirring constantly. Add to flour mixture; mix well. Beat in eggs on low speed for 30 seconds; beat on high for 3 minutes. Add enough remaining flour to form a soft dough. Turn onto a floured surface; knead until smooth and elastic, about 6-8 minutes. Divide dough into thirds. Knead cocoa into one-third of the dough (this may take 5-6 minutes). Shape into a ball. Shape remaining two-thirds dough into one ball. Place each ball in a lightly greased bowl, turning once to grease top. Cover and let rise in a warm place until doubled, about 1-1/4 hours. Punch dough down. Cover and let rest for 10 minutes. On a lightly floured surface, roll white dough into a 20-in. x 10-in. rectangle; repeat with chocolate dough. Place chocolate layer on top of white layer. Starting with long side, roll up jelly-roll style; press edges to seal seam. Cut into 20 slices; place in a greased 10-in. tube pan in about three layers. Cover and let rise until nearly doubled, about 30-40 minutes. Bake at 350° for 40-45 minutes or until lightly browned. Remove from pan immediately; cool on a wire rack. Combine sugar and milk; drizzle over bread. Sprinkle with nuts. **Yield:** 1 loaf.

VEGETABLE FRITTATA
Alice Parker, Moultrie, Georgia
(Pictured on page 12)

This fresh-tasting dish is an easy all-in-one meal. The bacon, eggs and hash browns make it hearty. The green broccoli and red paprika give it a look that fits the season.

   4 bacon strips, cut into 1/2-inch pieces
   2 cups frozen shredded hash browns, thawed
   1 cup chopped broccoli
  1/2 cup chopped green pepper
  1/2 cup chopped red onion
  1/2 to 1 teaspoon dried rosemary, crushed
   6 eggs
   3 tablespoons water
  1/2 teaspoon salt
  1/4 teaspoon pepper
  1/4 teaspoon paprika

In an 8-in. ovenproof skillet, cook the bacon until crisp. Drain, reserving 2 tablespoons drippings in the skillet. Remove bacon to paper towel. To the skillet, add hash browns, broccoli, green pepper, onion and rosemary; cover and cook over low heat until hash browns are golden brown and vegetables are tender, about 10 minutes. Remove from the heat and set aside. Beat eggs, water, salt and pepper; pour over hash browns. Top with bacon and paprika. Bake, uncovered, at 350° for 12-15 minutes or until eggs are completely set. **Yield:** 4-6 servings.

STRAWBERRY CHEESECAKE FRENCH TOAST
Darlene Markel, Sublimity, Oregon
(Pictured on page 12)

For a tempting breakfast dish that's more like dessert, try this! The rich filling between the French toast slices tastes like cheesecake. And who can resist sweet strawberries?

   1 carton (8 ounces) ricotta cheese
   3 tablespoons confectioners' sugar
   1 teaspoon vanilla extract
  16 slices French bread (1/2 inch thick)
   2 eggs
   1 cup milk
   2 cups sliced fresh *or* frozen strawberries
Additional confectioners' sugar *or* maple syrup
Hot cooked sausage links, optional

In a small bowl, combine ricotta, sugar and vanilla; mix well. Spread 2 tablespoons each on eight slices of bread; cover with remaining bread. In a bowl, beat eggs and milk; soak sandwiches for 1-2 minutes per side. Cook on a hot greased griddle for 5 minutes on each side or until golden brown and heated through. Serve with strawberries. Top with confectioners' sugar or syrup. Serve with sausages if desired. **Yield:** 4-6 servings.

BOUNTIFUL BRUNCH! Starting clockwise from top right: Citrus Sunshine Punch (p. 13), Vegetable Frittata (p. 11), Strawberry Cheesecake French Toast (p. 11), Any-Season Fruit Bowl (p. 13) and Cranberry Muffins (p. 13).

CITRUS SUNSHINE PUNCH
From the *Country Woman* Test Kitchen
(Pictured on page 12)

It's easy to be merry when sipping on this tangy punch. A cool, frothy glass of punch is a terrific way to wake up your taste buds on Christmas or any special day.

>   1 can (12 ounces) frozen lemonade concentrate, thawed
>   1 can (12 ounces) frozen limeade concentrate, thawed
>   1 can (12 ounces) frozen orange juice concentrate, thawed
>   2 quarts cold water
>   1 bottle (2 liters) ginger ale, chilled
> Ice cubes
>   1 quart orange sherbet

In a large container, combine concentrates with water; mix well. Chill. Just before serving, add ginger ale and ice cubes. Top with scoops of sherbet. **Yield:** 40 servings (about 1/2 cup each).

ANY-SEASON FRUIT BOWL
Frances Stevenson, McRae, Georgia
(Pictured on page 12)

A refreshing fruit salad like this one is a welcome addition to a winter meal. A hint of anise gives it real holiday flavor …and it looks gorgeous on a buffet table.

>   2 cups water
> 1-1/2 cups sugar
>   1/3 cup lime *or* lemon juice
>   1 teaspoon anise extract
>   1/2 teaspoon salt
>   3 oranges, peeled and sectioned
>   3 kiwifruit, peeled and sliced
>   2 grapefruit, peeled and sectioned
>   2 large apples, cubed
>   1 pint strawberries, sliced
>   1 pound green grapes
>   1 can (20 ounces) pineapple chunks, drained

In a medium saucepan, combine water, sugar, lime juice, anise and salt. Bring to a boil over medium heat; cook for 20 minutes, stirring occasionally. Remove from the heat; cover and refrigerate for 6 hours or overnight. Combine fruit in a large bowl; add dressing and toss to coat. Cover and chill for at least 1 hour. **Yield:** 16-18 servings.

CRANBERRY MUFFINS
Leona Luecking, West Burlington, Iowa
(Pictured on page 12)

I always make these delicately flavored muffins for the holidays. With tart ruby cranberries peeking out and a sugar-and-spice topping, they don't last long.

>   1/2 cup butter *or* margarine, softened
>   1 cup sugar
>   2 eggs
>   1 teaspoon vanilla extract
>   1 cup (8 ounces) sour cream
>   2 cups all-purpose flour
>   1 teaspoon baking powder
>   1/2 teaspoon baking soda
>   1/2 teaspoon ground nutmeg
>   1/4 teaspoon salt
>   1 cup chopped fresh *or* frozen cranberries
> TOPPING:
>   2 tablespoons sugar
>   1/8 teaspoon ground nutmeg

In a mixing bowl, cream butter and sugar. Add eggs and vanilla; mix well. Fold in sour cream. Combine flour, baking powder, baking soda, nutmeg and salt; stir into the creamed mixture just until moistened. Fold in cranberries. Fill greased or paper-lined muffin cups two-thirds full. Combine topping ingredients; sprinkle over muffins. Bake at 400° for 20-25 minutes or until muffins test done. Cool in pan 10 minutes; remove to a wire rack. **Yield:** 1 dozen.

APRICOT SAUSAGES
Christy Lacey-Igoe, Cape May, New Jersey

Here at the Sea Holly Bed & Breakfast, I have a simple way to dress up regular sausage links for the holidays—with a golden apricot sauce. This is one recipe that guests often request.

>   1 package (12 ounces) fresh pork sausage links
>   1/3 cup orange juice
>   2 tablespoons apricot preserves
> Orange slices, optional

In a medium skillet, brown sausages on all sides. Add enough water to cover. Bring to a boil over medium heat; cook for 10 minutes. Drain. Add juice and preserves. Reduce heat; cover and simmer for 30 minutes, turning sausages occasionally. Serve with a slotted spoon. Garnish with orange slices if desired. **Yield:** 6 servings.

SWISS BAKE
Maxine Kenning, Hutchinson, Minnesota

This creamy, comforting potato side dish has been a family favorite since my daughter got the recipe from a friend a dozen years ago. It's easy to fix using frozen hash browns.

>   1 package (26 ounces) frozen shredded hash browns, thawed
>   2 cups (8 ounces) shredded Swiss cheese
>   1 package (10 ounces) frozen chopped broccoli, thawed and well drained
>   2 cups whipping cream
>   1/2 cup chopped onion
>   1/2 cup butter *or* margarine, melted
>   1 teaspoon salt
>   1/4 teaspoon pepper

Combine all ingredients; pour into a greased 13-in. x 9-in. x 2-in. baking dish. Bake, uncovered, at 350° for 1 hour or until golden brown. **Yield:** 10-12 servings.

Christmas Breads

JULEKAGE
Carol Mead, Los Alamos, New Mexico
(Pictured on page 17)

When we lived in California, a friend made these for us at Christmas. Once we moved here, I found myself missing those light, moist loaves, dotted with candied fruit and blanketed with thick frosting. So I hunted up this recipe and started making them. The cardamom gives the bread a wonderfully distinctive flavor.

        2 packages (1/4 ounce *each*) active dry yeast
    1/2 cup plus 1 teaspoon sugar, *divided*
    1/2 cup warm water (110° to 115°)
    3/4 cup warm milk (110° to 115°)
    1/2 cup butter *or* margarine, softened
        1 egg
        1 teaspoon salt
    1/2 teaspoon ground cardamom
        5 to 5-1/2 cups all-purpose flour
1-1/2 cups chopped mixed candied fruit
    1/2 cup golden raisins
FROSTING:
        1 cup confectioners' sugar
        2 tablespoons butter *or* margarine, melted
        1 tablespoon milk
Red and green candied cherries

In a mixing bowl, dissolve yeast and 1 teaspoon sugar in water; let stand for 5 minutes. Add milk, butter, egg, salt, cardamom, 2-1/4 cups flour and remaining sugar. Beat until smooth. Stir in fruit, raisins and enough remaining flour to form a soft dough. Turn onto a floured surface; knead until smooth and elastic, about 6-8 minutes. Place in a greased bowl, turning once to grease top. Cover and let rise in a warm place until doubled, about 1-1/2 hours. Punch dough down; shape into two loaves; place in two greased 8-in. x 4-in. x 2-in. loaf pans. Cover and let rise until doubled, about 45 minutes. Bake at 350° for 35-40 minutes or until golden brown. Remove from pans and cool on wire racks. For frosting, combine sugar, butter and milk until smooth; spread over loaves. Decorate with cherries. **Yield:** 2 loaves.

MACADAMIA NUT MINI LOAVES
Kim Gilliland, Simi Valley, California
(Pictured on page 16)

While these loaves may be small, they have a big rich flavor. The macadamia nuts make them a special treat with tropical flair. Plus, they're so pretty with the toasted coconut topping.

        1 jar (3-1/2 ounces) macadamia nuts, *divided*
    1/3 cup flaked coconut
1-1/2 cups sugar, *divided*
    3/4 cup butter *or* margarine, softened
        2 eggs
        3 cups all-purpose flour

        1 teaspoon baking powder
    1/2 cup milk
        3 tablespoons lemon juice
        2 teaspoons grated lemon peel
1-1/2 teaspoons vanilla extract

Finely chop enough of the macadamia nuts to measure 1/3 cup; set aside. Coarsely chop remaining nuts; toss with coconut and 1 tablespoon sugar. Set aside. In a mixing bowl, cream butter and remaining sugar on high until fluffy. Add eggs; mix well. Combine flour and baking powder; add alternately with milk to creamed mixture. Stir in lemon juice and peel, vanilla and reserved finely chopped nuts. Spoon into six greased 4-1/2-in. x 2-1/2-in. x 1-1/2-in. loaf pans. Sprinkle with reserved coconut mixture. Bake at 325° for 50 minutes or until a toothpick inserted near the center comes out clean. Cool in pans for 10 minutes; remove and cool on a wire rack. **Yield:** 6 loaves. **Editor's Note:** If top begins to brown too quickly, cover loosely with heavy-duty aluminum foil.

EVELYN'S SOUR CREAM TWISTS
Linda Welch, North Platte, Nebraska
(Pictured on page 16)

"Evelyn" is my mother-in-law, who always keeps some of these terrific flaky twists in her freezer to serve in a pinch. They go quickly around our house—especially during the holidays.

        1 package (1/4 ounce) active dry yeast
    1/4 cup warm water (110° to 115°)
        3 cups all-purpose flour
1-1/2 teaspoons salt
    1/2 cup cold butter (no substitutes)
    1/2 cup shortening
        2 eggs
    1/2 cup sour cream
        3 teaspoons vanilla extract, *divided*
1-1/2 cups sugar

In a small bowl, dissolve yeast in water; let stand for 5 minutes. In a mixing bowl, combine flour and salt. Cut in butter and shortening until the mixture resembles coarse crumbs. Stir in eggs, sour cream, 1 teaspoon vanilla and the yeast mixture; mix thoroughly. Cover and refrigerate overnight. Combine sugar and remaining vanilla; lightly sprinkle 1/2 cup over a pastry cloth or countertop surface. On the sugared surface, roll half the dough into a 12-in. x 8-in. rectangle; refrigerate remaining dough. Sprinkle rolled dough with about 1 tablespoon of the sugar mixture. Fold rectangle into thirds. Give dough a quarter turn and repeat rolling, sugaring and folding two more times. Roll into a 12-in. x 8-in. rectangle. Cut into 4-in. x 1-in. strips; twist each strip two or three times. Place on chilled ungreased baking sheets. Repeat with remaining sugar mixture and dough. Bake at 375° for 12-14 minutes or until lightly browned. Immediately remove from pan and cool on wire racks. **Yield:** 4 dozen.

LEMON SCONES
Maureen De Garmo, Concord, California
(Pictured on pages 16 and 17)

These delicate scones are the perfect lightly sweet treat to serve with coffee or tea at any holiday get-together. It's a simple bread since, like biscuits, it doesn't require much kneading and there's no need to let the dough rise.

 2 cups all-purpose flour
1/4 cup sugar
 1 teaspoon baking powder
 1 teaspoon baking soda
1/4 teaspoon salt
1/2 cup cold butter *or* margarine
1/2 cup sour milk*
1-1/2 teaspoons grated lemon peel
Additional sugar

In a medium bowl, combine flour, sugar, baking powder, baking soda and salt. Cut in butter until mixture resembles fine crumbs. Add milk and lemon peel, stirring just until mixed. Turn onto a floured surface; knead gently six times. Shape into a ball. On a greased baking sheet, pat dough into a circle about 1/2 in. thick and 8-1/2 in. in diameter. Using a sharp knife, cut wedges in the dough, being careful not to cut all the way through. Sprinkle with sugar. Bake at 350° for 20-25 minutes or until edges are lightly browned. **Yield: 10-12 scones. *Editor's Note:** To sour milk, place 1-1/2 teaspoons white vinegar in a measuring cup. Add enough milk to equal 1/2 cup.

BRAN REFRIGERATOR ROLLS
Blanche Whytsell, Arnoldsburg, West Virginia
(Pictured on pages 16 and 17)

These golden rolls are very soft and tender. They're a delightful addition to any meal and convenient since you start them the day before you want to serve them.

1-3/4 cups boiling water
 1 cup all-bran cereal
 2 packages (1/4 ounce *each*) active dry yeast
1/4 cup warm water (110° to 115°)
1/2 cup shortening
1/2 cup sugar
1-1/2 teaspoons salt
 2 eggs
5-1/2 to 6 cups all-purpose flour

In a small bowl, combine boiling water and bran; set aside to cool. In another bowl, dissolve yeast in warm water; set aside. In a mixing bowl, cream shortening, sugar and salt; add eggs. Add yeast mixture and mix well. Add bran mixture and 2 cups flour, mixing well after each addition. Gradually add enough remaining flour to form a soft dough. Turn onto a lightly floured surface; knead until smooth and elastic, about 6-8 minutes. Place in a greased bowl, turning once to grease top. Cover and refrigerate overnight. Punch dough down; form into rolls. Place on greased baking sheets or in greased muffin cups. Cover and let rise until doubled, 1 to 1-1/2 hours. Bake at 375° for 15 minutes or until light brown. Remove from pan and cool on wire racks. **Yield: 3-1/2 dozen.**

FROSTED CARAMEL NUT BRAID
Paula Wiersma, Eastampton, New Jersey
(Pictured below)

It's become a Christmas-morning tradition for my husband, me and our two young children to munch on this scrumptious bread with its nutty filling while opening gifts. Since I make it ahead, I can also relax and enjoy the festivities.

 1 package (1/4 ounce) active dry yeast
1/4 cup warm water (110° to 115°)
 1 cup warm milk (110° to 115°)
 2 eggs
1/4 cup sugar
1/4 cup butter *or* margarine, softened
1-1/2 teaspoons salt
4-1/4 to 4-3/4 cups all-purpose flour
CARAMEL FILLING:
 1 cup chopped pecans
2/3 cup packed brown sugar
1/3 cup butter *or* margarine, softened
 2 tablespoons all-purpose flour
FROSTING:
1/3 cup butter *or* margarine, softened
 2 cups confectioners' sugar
1-1/2 teaspoons vanilla extract
 3 to 4 teaspoons water
1/4 cup chopped pecans

In a mixing bowl, dissolve yeast in water. Add milk, eggs, sugar, butter, salt and 2 cups flour; beat until smooth. Add enough remaining flour to form a soft but sticky dough. Do not knead. Cover and let rise in a warm place until doubled, about 1-1/2 hours. Beat 25 strokes with a spoon; turn onto a well-floured surface. Roll into a 16-in. x 12-in. rectangle. Combine filling ingredients with a fork; spread evenly over the dough. Cut dough lengthwise into three strips. Roll up jelly-roll style, beginning at a long end; pinch edges and ends to seal. Place three rolls diagonally, seam side down, on a foil-lined 15-in. x 10-in. x 1-in. baking pan. Braid ropes together gently (do not stretch); seal ends. Cover and let rise until doubled, about 1 hour. Bake at 350° for 25-30 minutes or until golden brown. Remove from pan and cool slightly on wire rack. For frosting, heat butter in a saucepan over low heat until golden brown; cool slightly. Stir in sugar and vanilla. Stir in enough water to make a spreadable consistency. Frost top of braid; immediately sprinkle with pecans. **Yield: 1 loaf.**

HOME-BAKED BREADS. Clockwise from top: Bran Refrigerator Rolls (p. 15), Julekage (p. 14), Lemon Scones (p. 15), Macadamia Nut Mini Loaves (p. 14) and Evelyn's Sour Cream Twists (p. 14).

CHERRY CHEESECAKE KOLACHES
Charlotte Sousek, Wahoo, Nebraska

I've been baking for 50 years. Since my granddaughter loves cherry cheesecake, I decided to try to put that kind of filling in kolaches—a traditional Czech pastry. It worked great, and now friends and relatives ask me to bring these kolaches to every get-together.

        1 package (1/4 ounce) active dry yeast
    1/4 cup warm water (110° to 115°)
        1 cup warm milk (110° to 115°)
    1/2 cup butter *or* margarine, softened
    1/2 cup sugar
    1/3 cup mashed potatoes (without added butter or
          milk)
        3 egg yolks
        1 teaspoon salt
        4 to 4-1/2 cups all-purpose flour
FILLING:
        2 packages (3 ounces *each*) cream cheese,
          softened
        1 egg
    1/3 cup sugar
    1/2 teaspoon grated lemon peel
    1/4 teaspoon vanilla extract
        1 can (21 ounces) cherry pie filling
GLAZE:
        1 cup confectioners' sugar
        1 tablespoon plus 1 teaspoon milk

In a mixing bowl, dissolve yeast in water. Add the milk, butter, sugar, potatoes, egg yolks and salt; beat until smooth. Add enough flour to make a very soft dough. Do not knead. Place in a greased bowl, turning once to grease top. Cover and let rise in a warm place until doubled, about 1 hour. Punch dough down; cover and let rest for 10 minutes. On a floured surface, roll about 1/4 cup of dough into a rope about 8-9 in. long. Tie in a knot; tuck one end on top and the other end under bottom of knot. Repeat for remaining dough. Place in greased 15-in. x 10-in. x 1-in. baking pans. Make a deep depression in each bun. For filling, beat cream cheese, egg, sugar, lemon peel and vanilla. Spoon 1 tablespoon into each bun. Make an indentation in filling; top each with 2 to 3 cherries from the pie filling (discard remaining cherry sauce or save for another use). Let rise until almost doubled, about 40 minutes. Bake at 400° for 12-15 minutes or until golden brown. Remove from pan and cool on wire racks. Combine glaze ingredients; drizzle over kolaches. **Yield:** 1-1/2 dozen.

CHEDDAR PULL-APART BREAD
Edwin Randall, South Beach, Oregon

As a retired chef, I know how homemade bread rounds out a meal. These crusty savory loaves have a wonderful cheese, onion and celery seed topping that makes them memorable.

        2 packages (1/4 ounce *each*) active dry yeast
        1 tablespoon sugar
        1 cup warm water (110° to 115°)
        2 tablespoons ground mustard
        1 teaspoon salt
    1-1/2 cups warm milk (110° to 115°)
        6 to 6-1/2 cups all-purpose flour
TOPPING:
    3/4 cup warm water (110° to 115°)
    1/2 cup dried minced onion
        1 cup (4 ounces) shredded cheddar cheese
        2 teaspoons celery seed
        1 egg, beaten

In a large mixing bowl, dissolve yeast and sugar in water; let stand for 10 minutes. Add mustard and salt; beat until smooth. Add milk and enough flour to form a soft dough. Turn onto a floured surface; knead until smooth and elastic, about 6-8 minutes. Place in a greased bowl, turning once to grease top. Cover and let rise in a warm place until doubled, about 45 minutes. Punch dough down and divide into fourths. Divide each portion into eight balls; place eight balls each in two greased 9-in. x 5-in. x 3-in. loaf pans. For topping, combine water and onion; let stand for 5 minutes. Add cheese and celery seed. Sprinkle half over dough in pans. Top with remaining dough balls and topping. Cover and let rise in a warm place until doubled, about 1 hour. Brush tops with egg. Bake at 375° for 30-35 minutes or until golden brown. Cool in pans for 10 minutes; remove from pan to wire rack to cool completely. **Yield:** 2 loaves.

CHRISTMAS STAR ROLLS
Ann Harrill, Reidsville, North Carolina

On a special day, preparing mouth-watering cinnamon rolls with a rich caramel sauce is a tempting way to treat family and friends. Using convenient hot roll mix makes it easy to do, and the pecans and candied cherries give the rolls a lovely look.

        1 package (16 ounces) hot roll mix
        2 tablespoons butter *or* margarine, melted
    1/2 cup sugar
        2 teaspoons ground cinnamon
    3/4 cup pecan halves
    3/4 cup candied cherry halves
GLAZE:
        2 cups packed brown sugar
    1/4 cup light corn syrup
        2 tablespoons butter *or* margarine

Prepare hot roll mix according to package directions. Turn onto a floured surface; knead until smooth and elastic, about 5 minutes. Cover and let rest for 5 minutes. Divide dough in half. Roll each half into a 1/4-in.-thick rectangle. Brush with butter. Combine sugar and cinnamon; sprinkle over dough. Roll up jelly-roll style, starting at a long end; pinch edges to seal seam. Cut each roll into eight equal pieces and set aside. Arrange pecans and cherries in two greased 8-in. round pans or 6-cup ring molds. Combine glaze ingredients in a medium saucepan; cook and stir over low heat until the butter is melted and the mixture is well blended. Pour glaze over pecans and cherries; top with rolls. Cover and let rise in a warm place until doubled, about 30-45 minutes. Bake at 350° for 20-25 minutes or until golden brown. Immediately invert pans onto platters and let glaze drizzle over rolls. **Yield:** 16 rolls.

PUMPKIN SWIRL BREAD
Cindy May, Troy, Michigan

This combination of pumpkin, nuts and dates makes a flavorful bread with a beautiful golden look. The surprise inside—a rich creamy swirl—is almost like a luscious layer of cheesecake in each slice.

FILLING:
- 2 packages (8 ounces *each*) cream cheese, softened
- 1/4 cup sugar
- 1 egg
- 1 tablespoon milk

BREAD:
- 3 cups sugar
- 2 cups canned *or* cooked pumpkin
- 1 cup vegetable oil
- 1 cup water
- 4 eggs
- 4 cups all-purpose flour
- 4 teaspoons pumpkin pie spice
- 2 teaspoons baking soda
- 1-1/2 teaspoons ground cinnamon
- 1 teaspoon baking powder
- 1 teaspoon ground nutmeg
- 1 teaspoon salt
- 1/2 teaspoon ground cloves
- 1 cup chopped walnuts
- 1 cup raisins
- 1/2 cup chopped dates

In a small mixing bowl, beat cream cheese, sugar, egg and milk; set aside. In a large mixing bowl, beat sugar, pumpkin, oil, water and eggs. Combine dry ingredients; gradually add to pumpkin mixture and mix well. Stir in nuts, raisins and dates. Pour half of the batter into three greased and floured 8-in. x 4-in. x 2-in. loaf pans. Spoon filling over batter. Cover filling completely with remaining batter. Bake at 350° for 65-70 minutes or until a toothpick inserted near the center comes out clean. Cool for 10 minutes; remove from pan and cool completely on a wire rack. Wrap in foil; refrigerate until ready to serve. **Yield:** 3 loaves.

CONFETTI BUBBLE RING
Virginia Krites, Cridersville, Ohio

My daughters made this ring when they were in 4-H, and we've enjoyed it for many years. Handy refrigerated biscuits get a holiday spin combined with other tasty, colorful ingredients.

- 1/2 pound sliced bacon, diced
- 1/4 cup chopped onion
- 1/4 cup grated Parmesan cheese
- 1/4 cup chopped green pepper
- 2 tubes (7-1/2 ounces *each*) refrigerated biscuits
- 1/3 cup butter *or* margarine, melted

In a skillet, cook bacon until crisp; drain. Place in a bowl; add onion, cheese and green pepper. Cut biscuits into quarters; add to bacon mixture. Add butter and toss to coat. Pour into a greased 10-in. tube pan. Bake at 350° for 30 minutes. **Yield:** 8-10 servings.

SUNSHINE MUFFINS
Joyce Minge Johns, Jacksonville, Florida

These hearty muffins are packed with goodies like pineapple, coconut, raisins and pecans. We enjoy them with coffee on Christmas morning. In fact, my family likes them so much that I now also make them for Thanksgiving breakfast.

- 1-1/2 cups all-purpose flour
- 2/3 cup sugar
- 1 teaspoon baking powder
- 1 teaspoon baking soda
- 1 teaspoon ground cinnamon
- 1/4 teaspoon salt
- 2 eggs
- 1 cup finely shredded carrots
- 2/3 cup vegetable oil
- 1/2 cup crushed pineapple, drained
- 1/2 cup flaked coconut
- 1/2 cup raisins
- 1/2 cup chopped pecans

In a bowl, combine flour, sugar, baking powder, baking soda, cinnamon and salt. In another bowl, beat eggs; add carrots, oil and pineapple. Stir into dry ingredients just until moistened. Fold in coconut, raisins and pecans. Fill greased or paper-lined muffin cups two-thirds full. Bake at 350° for 20-25 minutes or until muffins test done. Cool in pan 10 minutes; remove from pan and cool on wire rack. **Yield:** about 1 dozen.

EGGNOG BREAD
Sue Boudreau, Chicago, Illinois

I got this recipe from an old friend. It combines two holiday favorites—eggnog and fruit-and-nut bread. My children look forward to me making it each Christmas, plus I give loaves as gifts to my co-workers.

- 4-3/4 cups all-purpose flour
- 3/4 cup sugar
- 4 teaspoons baking powder
- 1/2 teaspoon salt
- 1/2 teaspoon ground nutmeg
- 2-3/4 cups eggnog*
- 2 eggs
- 1/2 cup vegetable oil
- 3/4 cup chopped dried apricots
- 3/4 cup chopped pecans

ICING:
- 2/3 cup confectioners' sugar
- 1 tablespoon eggnog*

In a large bowl, combine flour, sugar, baking powder, salt and nutmeg. In a small bowl, combine eggnog, eggs and oil; add to dry ingredients, stirring just until moistened. Fold in apricots and pecans. Pour into two 8-in. x 4-in. x 2-in. or four 5-3/4-in. x 3-in. x 2-in. greased loaf pans. Bake at 350° for 50-60 minutes or until a toothpick inserted near the center comes out clean. Cool in pan for 10 minutes; remove to a wire rack to cool completely. Combine icing ingredients until smooth; spread over bread. **Yield:** 2 regular loaves or 4 mini loaves. ***Editor's Note:** This recipe was tested with commercially prepared eggnog.

Appetizers

CHICKEN WINGS WITH SPICY APRICOT SAUCE
Shirley Eckert, Crestline, Ohio
(Pictured on page 21)

Everyone gobbles these up at Christmas potlucks! My mother gave me the recipe for this anytime appetizer with its flavorful sweet-and-sour sauce.

        3 dozen whole chicken wings
1-1/2 cups cornstarch
    1 tablespoon baking powder
1-1/2 teaspoons salt
    1/2 teaspoon pepper
    1/2 teaspoon sugar
      3 eggs, beaten
Cooking oil for deep-fat frying
SAUCE:
      1 cup (3 ounces) dried apricots
1-1/4 cups water
      2 tablespoons sugar
      2 tablespoons cider vinegar
      2 tablespoons honey
    1/8 to 1/4 teaspoon cayenne pepper

Cut chicken wings into three sections; discard wing tip section. In a shallow bowl or large resealable plastic bag, combine cornstarch, baking powder, salt, pepper and sugar. Dip chicken pieces in eggs, then coat generously with cornstarch mixture. In an electric skillet or deep-fat fryer, heat oil to 350°. Fry chicken wings, a few at a time, for about 9 minutes or until juices run clear. Drain on paper towels. Keep warm. Meanwhile, combine apricots and water in a saucepan; bring to a boil. Reduce heat; cover and simmer until apricots are tender. Transfer to a blender or food processor. Add sugar, vinegar, honey and cayenne; puree until smooth. Cool slightly. Serve with chicken wings. **Yield:** 6 dozen. **Editor's Note:** Sauce can be made ahead, covered and refrigerated. Reheat and thin with a little water if necessary.

SALMON CANAPES
Dorothy Anderson, Ottawa, Kansas
(Pictured on page 21)

This appealing appetizer, with its delicate smoked salmon taste and dash of holiday color, is simply irresistible!

    1 can (7-1/2 ounces) red salmon, drained, skin
      and bones removed
    2 tablespoons minced celery
    2 tablespoons minced green onions with tops
    3 tablespoons mayonnaise
  1/2 teaspoon lemon juice
  1/4 teaspoon salt
  1/8 teaspoon pepper
  1/8 teaspoon liquid smoke, optional
    1 small cucumber, thinly sliced

Snack rye bread, toast *or* crackers
Fresh dill *or* parsley sprigs *and/or* sliced pimientos

In a bowl, combine salmon, celery and onions. Add mayonnaise, lemon juice, salt, pepper and liquid smoke if desired; mix well. Cover and chill at least 1 hour. Just before serving, place cucumber slices on bread or crackers and top with salmon mixture. Garnish with dill, parsley and/or pimientos. **Yield:** 1 cup spread.

STRAWBERRY DIP
Doris Soliwoda, La Mesa, California
(Pictured on page 21)

Fresh and fruity, this versatile dip lends a hint of summertime to Yuletide. It's light in taste and pretty in holiday pink.

      1 package (8 ounces) cream cheese, softened
  1/2 cup sour cream
      1 carton (6 ounces) lemon yogurt
  1/4 cup mashed strawberries
      3 tablespoons honey
      1 tablespoon maple syrup
Fresh fruit

In a mixing bowl, beat cream cheese and sour cream until smooth. Add yogurt, strawberries, honey and syrup; mix well. Refrigerate for at least 4 hours. Stir before serving. Use fruit for dipping. **Yield:** about 2 cups.

CRAB-STUFFED CHERRY TOMATOES
Marcia Keckhaver, Burlington, Wisconsin
(Pictured on page 21)

For a little something special, I include these petite pleasers on the menu of our holiday parties. Our six children and 15 grandkids eat them up warm and juicy from the oven.

      1 pint cherry tomatoes
      1 can (6 ounces) crabmeat, drained, flaked and
        cartilage removed
  1/2 cup diced green pepper
      2 green onions, diced
      2 tablespoons Italian-seasoned bread crumbs
      1 teaspoon cider *or* white wine vinegar
  1/2 teaspoon dried parsley flakes
  1/4 teaspoon dill weed
  1/8 teaspoon salt, optional

Cut a thin slice off tops of tomatoes and carefully scoop out insides; invert on paper towels to drain. In a small bowl, combine remaining ingredients; mix well. Stuff tomatoes; place in an ungreased 13-in. x 9-in. x 2-in. baking dish. Bake, uncovered, at 350° for 8-10 minutes or until heated through. Serve warm. **Yield:** about 1-1/2 dozen.

TEMPTING APPETIZERS. Clockwise from top right: Chicken Wings with Spicy Apricot Sauce (p. 20), Crab-Stuffed Cherry Tomatoes (p. 20), Salmon Canapes (p. 20), Strawberry Dip (p. 20) and Holiday Eggnog (p. 22).

HOLIDAY EGGNOG
Pat Waymire, Yellow Springs, Ohio
(Pictured on page 21)

This classic Christmas beverage is so smooth and creamy that you can count on friends and family coming back for seconds! Our gang loves it sprinkled with nutmeg.

        12 eggs
1-1/2 cups sugar
    1/2 teaspoon salt
      2 quarts milk, *divided*
      2 tablespoons vanilla extract
      1 teaspoon ground nutmeg
      2 cups whipping cream
Additional whipped cream and nutmeg, optional

In a heavy 4-qt. saucepan, whisk together eggs, sugar and salt. Gradually add 1 qt. of milk. Cook over low heat, stirring constantly, until a thermometer reads 160°, about 25 minutes. Pour into a large bowl; stir in vanilla, nutmeg and remaining milk. Place bowl in an ice-water bath; stir frequently until mixture is cool. If mixture separates, process in a blender until smooth. Cover and refrigerate for at least 3 hours. When ready to serve, beat cream in a mixing bowl on high until soft peaks form; whisk gently into cooled mixture. Pour into a chilled 5-qt. punch bowl. If desired, top with dollops of whipped cream and sprinkle with nutmeg. **Yield:** 18 servings (about 3/4 cup each).

SPINACH SQUARES
Patricia Kile, Greentown, Pennsylvania

Even people who don't care for spinach can't pass up these satisfying squares. They're a hit as a deliciously different vegetable side dish as well.

      2 tablespoons butter *or* margarine, melted,
        divided
      1 cup milk
      3 eggs
      1 cup all-purpose flour
      1 teaspoon baking powder
    3/4 teaspoon salt
    1/2 teaspoon dried oregano
    1/4 teaspoon pepper
    1/4 teaspoon dried basil
    1/4 teaspoon dried thyme
      2 packages (10 ounces *each*) frozen chopped
        spinach, thawed and squeezed dry
      2 cups (8 ounces) shredded cheddar cheese
      2 cups (8 ounces) shredded Monterey Jack cheese
      1 cup chopped onion
Sliced pimientos, optional

Brush the bottom and sides of a 13-in. x 9-in. x 2-in. baking dish with 1 tablespoon butter; set aside. In a mixing bowl, combine remaining butter and the next nine ingredients; mix well. Stir in the spinach, cheeses and onion. Spread in pan. Bake, uncovered, at 350° for 30-35 minutes or until a toothpick inserted near the center comes out clean and edges are lightly browned. Cut into squares. Garnish with pimientos if desired. **Yield:** 32 appetizers or 16-20 side-dish servings.

CHEESE STRAWS
Edna Mae Dark, Clinton, Missouri

A fellow schoolteacher gave me this recipe that's since become a family favorite. It's also popular at various church functions featuring eat-with-your-fingers fare.

      4 cups (1 pound) shredded cheddar cheese
    1/2 cup butter *or* margarine
      2 cups all-purpose flour
      1 teaspoon cayenne pepper

Bring cheese and butter to room temperature; mix them together by hand. Add flour and cayenne; mix well. Use a cookie press with a star or zigzag end plate to make strips on ungreased baking sheets. Bake at 350° for 12-14 minutes or until golden brown and as crisp as desired. **Yield:** 10 dozen.

FIESTA PINWHEELS
Diane Martin, Brown Deer, Wisconsin

Whenever I serve these make-ahead appetizers, they disappear fast. When a friend at the office shared them with me, I knew in one bite I'd be bringing her recipe home for the holidays.

      1 package (8 ounces) cream cheese, softened
    1/2 cup sour cream
    1/4 cup picante sauce
      2 tablespoons taco seasoning mix
Dash garlic powder
      1 can (4-1/2 ounces) chopped ripe olives, drained
      1 can (4 ounces) chopped green chilies
      1 cup (4 ounces) finely shredded cheddar cheese
    1/2 cup thinly sliced green onions
      8 flour tortillas (10 inches)
Salsa

In a small mixing bowl, beat cream cheese, sour cream, picante sauce, taco seasoning and garlic powder until smooth. Stir in olives, chilies, cheese and onions. Spread about 1/2 cup on each tortilla. Roll up jelly-roll style; wrap in plastic wrap. Refrigerate for 2 hours or overnight. Slice into 1-in. pieces. Serve with salsa. **Yield:** about 5 dozen. **Editor's Note:** Pinwheels may be prepared ahead and frozen. Thaw in the refrigerator.

PIZZA BREAD
Carla Hodenfield, Mandan, North Dakota

This moist, cheesy bread is a fun appetizer that I also use to complement Italian meals and main-dish salads.

      2 teaspoons yellow cornmeal
      1 tube (12 ounces) refrigerated biscuits
    1/2 cup pizza sauce
    3/4 cup shredded mozzarella cheese

Sprinkle cornmeal on the bottom of a greased 8-in. square baking pan. Cut each biscuit into quarters; toss with pizza sauce. Place in pan; sprinkle with cheese. Bake at 400° for 14 minutes or until golden brown. **Yield:** 8-10 servings.

CHILI CUPS
Diane Hixon, Niceville, Florida

Nothing tickles appetites quicker than these spicy tidbits. It's like eating chili in a muffin. I like assembling and freezing them ahead of time to beat the Christmas rush in my kitchen.

        1 pound ground beef
        1 medium green pepper, diced
        1 medium onion, diced
        3 garlic cloves, minced
        1 can (8 ounces) tomato sauce
        2 tablespoons water
    1/2 teaspoon salt
    1/2 to 1 teaspoon ground cumin
    1/2 teaspoon dried oregano
    1/4 teaspoon celery seed
    1/4 teaspoon dill weed
    1/8 to 1/4 teaspoon cayenne pepper
        2 loaves (1 pound *each*) sliced Italian bread
Grated Parmesan cheese

In a large skillet, brown beef, green pepper, onion and garlic; drain. Stir in tomato sauce, water and seasonings. Bring to a boil over medium heat. Reduce heat; cover and simmer for 30 minutes, stirring occasionally. Meanwhile, cut 2-1/2-in. circles from bread slices using a biscuit cutter. Press the circles into greased miniature muffin cups. Bake at 400° for 5-6 minutes or until lightly toasted. Remove from tins and cool on wire racks. Fill each bread cup with about 1 tablespoon chili mixture; sprinkle with Parmesan cheese. Broil for 2-3 minutes or until cheese is golden brown. **Yield:** about 5 dozen. ***Editor's Note:** Some slices of bread will yield two 2-1/2-in. circles and some slices only one. There may be bread slices left over.

ZIPPY CHEESE LOG
Evangeline Rew, Manassas, Virginia

Due to popular demand, my pretty cheese log has become a tasty tradition at our women's Christmas brunch. As soon as the ladies try a bite, I start getting requests for the recipe.

        2 packages (8 ounces *each*) cream cheese, softened
        1 cup small-curd cottage cheese
        1 envelope (1 ounce) Parmesan Italian salad
          dressing mix
        4 tablespoons minced fresh parsley, *divided*
    1/2 cup minced fully cooked ham
    1/2 cup chopped walnuts
Assorted crackers

In a mixing bowl, beat cream cheese, cottage cheese and salad dressing mix until smooth. Line the bottom and sides of a 13-in. x 9-in. x 2-in. pan with waxed paper. Spread cheese mixture evenly in pan. Cover and refrigerate for 1 hour. Remove waxed paper with cheese from pan. Sprinkle 2 tablespoons parsley in a 13-in. x 1-in. strip 1/2 in. from one long edge. Sprinkle ham over remaining cheese mixture. Starting with parsley edge, carefully roll up jelly-roll style. Combine walnuts and remaining parsley; roll log in parsley mixture. Cut log in half; wrap and refrigerate for at least 4 hours. Serve with crackers. **Yield:** 2 cheese logs (about 1-3/4 cups each).

MUSTARD DIP
Elsie Hyer, Souderton, Pennsylvania

Some like it hot—but others prefer a mustard that's mildly sweet. This easy-to-make food gift can be fixed either way. It really keeps its "zip" in the refrigerator.

        1 can (14 ounces) sweetened condensed milk
    1/4 cup ground *or* prepared mustard*
        3 tablespoons prepared horseradish
        1 tablespoon Worcestershire sauce

In a bowl, combine all ingredients until smooth (mustard will thicken as it stands). Store in the refrigerator. **Yield:** 1-1/2 cups. ***Editor's Note:** To make hot and zippy dip for pretzels and egg rolls, use ground mustard. To make a milder, sweeter sauce that's very good with ham and turkey, use prepared mustard.

HOT BUTTERED LEMONADE
Jennifer Jones, Springfield, Missouri

Since my husband had fond childhood memories of this winter warmer-upper, I simmered up a batch. It's delicious, simple to prepare for drop-in guests and sets a soothing holiday mood.

        3 cups water
    3/4 cup fresh lemon juice
    2/3 cup sugar
    1-1/2 teaspoons grated lemon peel
        1 tablespoon butter *or* margarine
        4 cinnamon sticks (4 inches), optional

In a saucepan over medium heat, simmer water, lemon juice, sugar and lemon peel until sugar is dissolved. Pour into mugs; dot each with butter. Serve with a cinnamon stick if desired. **Yield:** 4 servings (about 1 cup each).

STUFFED MUSHROOMS
Bryan Anderson, Granite Falls, Minnesota

These scrumptious mushroom appetizers—from my grandmother's recipe—are perfect for serving at special-occasion dinners and birthdays.

        16 to 18 large fresh whole mushrooms
        1 small onion, chopped
        1 garlic clove, minced
        2 tablespoons butter *or* margarine
        8 butter-flavored crackers, crushed
        3 ounces pepperoni *or* summer sausage, finely
          chopped
    1/4 cup grated Parmesan cheese
        1 tablespoon minced fresh parsley
    1/8 teaspoon pepper

Remove stems from mushrooms; set caps aside. Mince the stems. In a skillet over medium heat, saute stems, onion and garlic in butter until soft. Remove from the heat and stir in remaining ingredients. Firmly stuff into mushroom caps; place on a greased baking sheet. Bake at 375° for 15-20 minutes or until tender. **Yield:** about 1-1/2 dozen.

Christmas Dinner

HOLIDAY PEAS AND RICE
Patricia Rutherford, Winchester, Illinois
(Pictured below)

With all the fuss that goes into holiday meals, it's nice to find a side dish like this that's both satisfying and simple. The pimientos and peas nestle among rice delightfully seasoned with sage and chicken broth.

    1/2 cup uncooked long grain rice
    1/8 teaspoon rubbed sage
    2 tablespoons butter *or* margarine
    1 can (14-1/2 ounces) chicken broth
    1 cup fresh *or* frozen peas
    2 tablespoons diced pimientos

In a saucepan, saute rice and sage in butter until rice is lightly browned. Add broth; bring to a boil. Reduce heat; cover and simmer for 20 minutes. Add peas; simmer, uncovered, 10 minutes longer or until heated through, stirring occasionally. Stir in pimientos. **Yield:** 4-6 servings.

ALMOND RICE WITH RASPBERRY SAUCE
Bonnie Wehrman, Ambrose, North Dakota
(Pictured on page 26)

It simply wouldn't be Christmas in our family without this old-fashioned dessert. Cool and creamy, it looks beautiful drizzled with the tart raspberry sauce.

       5 cups water, *divided*
       2 cups uncooked long grain rice
       2 teaspoons salt
    2-1/2 cups milk
       1 cup sugar
       1 cup slivered almonds, toasted
     1/4 teaspoon almond extract
       3 tablespoons cornstarch
       2 packages (10 ounces *each*) frozen sweetened
         raspberries, thawed
       2 tablespoons lemon juice
       2 cups whipping cream
    Fresh mint, optional

In a large saucepan over medium heat, bring 4 cups of water, rice and salt to a boil. Reduce heat; cover and simmer for 15 minutes or until rice is tender and liquid is absorbed. Stir in milk and sugar. Bring to a boil over medium heat; reduce heat and simmer, uncovered, until milk is absorbed and rice is creamy. Remove from the heat; stir in almonds and extract. Cool slightly; cover and chill. Meanwhile, in another saucepan, combine cornstarch and remaining water; add raspberries. Bring to a boil over medium heat; boil and stir for 2 minutes or until thickened. Remove from the heat; stir in lemon juice. Cover and chill. Just before serving, whip cream until soft peaks form; fold into rice mixture. Spoon into individual serving dishes and top with raspberry sauce. Garnish with mint if desired. **Yield:** 8-10 servings.

HAM SLICE WITH PINEAPPLE-ORANGE SAUCE
Ruth Andrewson, Leavenworth, Washington
(Pictured on page 27)

A juicy ham slice is just as tasty as a whole ham, and it's easier and faster to prepare. Plus, topped with golden pineapple sauce, this dish is so elegant on the table.

       1 fully cooked ham slice (about 1 inch thick and 2
         pounds)
       1 tablespoon butter *or* margarine
       1 can (8 ounces) unsweetened sliced pineapple
     1/3 cup orange juice
       3 tablespoons brown sugar
       2 teaspoons cornstarch
       1 teaspoon cider *or* white wine vinegar
    Dash ground ginger

In a skillet, brown ham in butter. Place in a greased 13-in. x 9-in. x 2-in. baking dish. Drain pineapple, reserving juice; set juice aside. Place pineapple over ham; set aside. In a saucepan, combine orange juice, brown sugar, cornstarch, vinegar, ginger and reserved pineapple juice; mix well. Bring to a boil over medium heat; boil and stir for 2 minutes or until thickened. Pour over ham and pineapple. Bake, uncovered, at 350° for 25-30 minutes or until ham is heated through. **Yield:** 6-8 servings.

CRANBERRY SWEET POTATO BAKE
Patricia Kile, Greentown, Pennsylvania
(Pictured on page 27)

Sweet potatoes and tart cranberries are a feast for the eyes as well as the palate in this appealing side dish.

1-1/2 pounds sweet potatoes
1-1/2 cups fresh *or* frozen cranberries
  2/3 cup sugar
  1/3 cup orange juice
   1 teaspoon salt
   1 tablespoon butter *or* margarine
1-1/2 cups granola cereal

In a large saucepan, cover sweet potatoes with water; bring to a boil. Reduce heat; cover and simmer for 30 minutes or until tender. Drain and cool. Peel potatoes; cut into 1-in. pieces. Combine cranberries, sugar, orange juice and salt; place half in a greased 11-in. x 7-in. x 2-in. baking dish. Top with half of the sweet potatoes. Repeat layers. Dot with butter. Cover and bake at 350° for 25 minutes or until cranberries are tender. Uncover and sprinkle with granola; return to the oven for 10 minutes. **Yield:** 6-8 servings.

BROCCOLI ARTICHOKE CASSEROLE
Sue Braunschweig, Delafield, Wisconsin
(Pictured on page 26)

A creamy mellow sauce draped over bold-tasting broccoli and artichokes makes this a great addition to any meal.

   3 packages (10 ounces *each*) frozen broccoli
     spears, thawed and drained
   2 cans (14 ounces *each*) artichoke hearts, drained
1-1/2 cups mayonnaise
  1/2 cup butter *or* margarine
  1/2 cup grated Parmesan cheese
   4 teaspoons lemon juice
  1/2 teaspoon celery salt
  1/2 cup slivered almonds, optional
   2 tablespoons diced pimientos, optional

Arrange broccoli and artichokes in a greased shallow 2-1/2-qt. baking dish; set aside. In a saucepan, combine mayonnaise, butter, cheese, lemon juice and celery salt; cook and stir over low heat until butter is melted and sauce is heated through (do not boil). Pour over broccoli and artichokes. Sprinkle with almonds and pimientos if desired. Bake, uncovered, at 350° for 30-40 minutes or until broccoli is crisp-tender. **Yield:** 8-10 servings.

CRANBERRY-GLAZED PORK ROAST
Theresa Pearson, Ogilvie, Minnesota
(Pictured on page 26)

My family loves pork prepared in this festive way. You'll find that this succulent roast, with its tangy ruby glaze, is an entree that you, too, will be proud to serve at the holidays year after year.

   1 boneless pork loin roast (3-1/2 to 4 pounds)
  12 small whole onions
   1 can (16 ounces) whole-berry cranberry sauce
  1/4 cup orange juice
   2 teaspoons cornstarch
  1/2 to 1 teaspoon grated orange peel
  1/4 teaspoon ground cinnamon
  1/8 teaspoon salt

Place roast, fat side up, in a greased roasting pan. Bake, uncovered, at 325° for 45 minutes. Place onions around roast; cover and bake for 30 minutes. Meanwhile, in a saucepan, combine cranberry sauce, orange juice, cornstarch, orange peel, cinnamon and salt; mix well. Bring to a boil over medium heat; boil and stir for 2 minutes or until thickened. Spoon 3/4 cup over roast and onions; set remaining sauce aside. Bake, basting occasionally, 30-45 minutes longer or until a meat thermometer reads 160°-170° and onions are tender. Let stand 15 minutes before slicing. Heat reserved sauce; serve with roast and onions. **Yield:** 12-14 servings.

OVERNIGHT ROLLS
Dorothy Yagodich, Charleroi, Pennsylvania
(Pictured on page 27)

I'm pleased to share the recipe for these light and tender rolls, which I've made for 25 years. I once served them to a woman who'd been in the restaurant business for half a century. She said they were the best rolls she'd ever tasted.

   1 package (1/4 ounce) active dry yeast
  1/2 cup plus 3/4 teaspoon sugar, *divided*
1-1/3 cups plus 3 tablespoons warm water (110°
     to 115°), *divided*
  1/3 cup vegetable oil
   1 egg
   1 teaspoon salt
4-3/4 to 5-1/4 cups all-purpose flour
Melted butter *or* margarine, optional

In a mixing bowl, dissolve yeast and 3/4 teaspoon sugar in 3 tablespoons water. Add remaining sugar and water, oil, egg, salt and 2 cups flour; mix well. Add enough remaining flour to form a soft dough. Turn onto a floured surface; knead until smooth and elastic, about 6-8 minutes. Place in a greased bowl, turning once to grease top. Cover and let rise in a warm place until doubled, about 1 hour. Punch dough down. Shape into 20 rolls. Place on a greased baking sheet; cover and refrigerate overnight. Allow rolls to sit at room temperature for 15 minutes before baking. Bake at 375° for 12-15 minutes or until lightly browned. Brush with butter if desired. Remove to wire racks to cool. **Yield:** 20 rolls.

YULETIDE DINNER! Clockwise from top right: Overnight Rolls (p. 25), Cranberry Sweet Potato Bake (p. 25), Ham Slice with Pineapple-Orange Sauce (p. 24), Almond Rice with Raspberry Sauce (p. 24), Broccoli Artichoke Casserole (p. 25) and Cranberry-Glazed Pork Roast (p. 25).

CHERRY COLA SALAD
Betty Aman, Center, North Dakota

This tempting gelatin salad has a big cherry flavor and a fun zing from the cola. My two small children are always happy to see this salad on the table. We think it tastes great with or without the whipped topping.

    1 package (6 ounces) cherry gelatin
1-1/2 cups boiling water
1-1/2 cups carbonated cola beverage
    1 can (21 ounces) cherry pie filling
Whipped topping, optional

Dissolve gelatin in water. Add cola and pie filling; mix well. Pour into an 8-in. square baking dish. Refrigerate until firm. Garnish with whipped topping if desired. **Yield:** 8-10 servings.

LAYERED VEGETABLE LOAF
Norma Valles, Bentonville, Arkansas

I receive many compliments on my out-of-the-ordinary side dish that features fluffy layers of eggs, cheese and vegetables topped with a creamy sauce. Even non-vegetable fans like this loaf.

FIRST LAYER:
    2 eggs, beaten
    1 cup chopped cooked broccoli
1/2 cup shredded cheddar cheese
    1 tablespoon butter *or* margarine, melted
1/4 teaspoon onion salt
SECOND LAYER:
    2 eggs, beaten
    1 cup cooked rice
1/2 cup shredded mozzarella cheese
1/2 cup chopped sweet red pepper
    1 tablespoon butter *or* margarine, melted
1/4 teaspoon onion salt
THIRD LAYER:
    2 eggs, beaten
    1 cup mashed cooked carrots
1/2 cup shredded cheddar cheese
    1 tablespoon butter *or* margarine, melted
1/4 teaspoon onion salt
SAUCE:
    2 tablespoons butter *or* margarine
    2 tablespoons all-purpose flour
    1 cup milk
1/4 teaspoon onion salt
1/8 teaspoon pepper

Combine first layer ingredients; pour into a greased 8-in. x 4-in. x 2-in. loaf pan. Combine second layer ingredients and spread over first layer. Combine third layer ingredients and spread over second layer. Bake at 300° for 65-75 minutes or until a knife inserted near the center comes out clean. Run a knife around edges to loosen; cool in pan to room temperature. For sauce, melt butter in a small saucepan; blend in flour until smooth. Gradually add milk, onion salt and pepper. Bring to a boil over medium heat; boil and stir for 2 minutes or until thickened. Unmold loaf onto a serving platter; serve with sauce. **Yield:** 8-10 servings.

CHRISTMAS CHICKEN CORDON BLEU
Vickie Lemos, Modesto, California

Christmas Eve wouldn't be complete without my dad's chicken cordon bleu! My husband tries all year to talk Dad into also making this scrumptious main dish for other occasions. It's a definite family favorite.

    6 boneless skinless chicken breast halves
    3 thin slices fully cooked ham, halved
    3 slices Swiss cheese, halved
1/2 cup all-purpose flour
1/2 teaspoon salt
1/4 teaspoon paprika
    1 egg
    2 tablespoons milk
3/4 cup dry bread crumbs
    3 tablespoons butter *or* margarine
    1 cup chicken broth
    2 tablespoons dried parsley flakes
Hot cooked rice
    1 can (10-3/4 ounces) condensed cream of chicken soup, undiluted
1/2 cup sour cream

Flatten chicken breasts to 1/4-in. thickness; top each with one piece of ham and one piece of cheese. Fold chicken around ham and cheese; secure with toothpicks. In a shallow bowl, combine flour, salt and paprika. In another bowl, beat egg and milk. Dredge chicken in flour mixture, dip in egg mixture, then roll in bread crumbs. In a large skillet over medium heat, brown chicken in butter. Add broth and parsley. Cover and simmer over medium-low heat for 50-60 minutes or until chicken juices run clear. Remove toothpicks. Place rice on a serving platter; top with chicken and keep warm. In the same skillet, combine soup and sour cream; heat through but do not boil. Pour over chicken and rice. **Yield:** 6 servings.

CRANBERRY CHUTNEY
Linda Shaffer, Crossville, Tennessee

The apples give my crimson chutney a pleasant crunch. I especially like this recipe because I can make it weeks ahead.

3-1/2 cups (12 ounces) fresh *or* frozen cranberries
    1 cup sugar
    1 cup water
1/2 cup packed brown sugar
1/2 cup raisins
    2 teaspoons ground cinnamon
1-1/2 teaspoons ground ginger
1/2 teaspoon ground cloves
1/4 teaspoon ground allspice
    1 cup chopped peeled apples

In a large saucepan over medium heat, combine the first nine ingredients. Cook, uncovered, for 15 minutes, stirring occasionally. Add apples. Reduce heat; cover and simmer for 10 minutes. Pour into jars or plastic containers; cover and refrigerate up to 3 weeks. Do not freeze. **Yield:** 3-1/2 cups.

POTATO CHEESE CASSEROLE
Jane Luxem, Green Bay, Wisconsin

This rich flavorful side dish is a Christmas tradition at our house. Plain potatoes are the start, but they get dressed up with a creamy cheese sauce and colorful ingredients like peppers and chives.

 4 pounds potatoes, peeled
 1 package (8 ounces) cream cheese, softened
 1/2 cup butter *or* margarine, softened
 1/4 cup milk
 1 to 1-1/4 teaspoons salt
 1/4 teaspoon pepper
 1 cup chopped green pepper
 1/2 cup shredded cheddar cheese
 1/2 cup grated Parmesan cheese
 1/2 cup snipped chives
 1 jar (2 ounces) diced pimientos, drained

Cook potatoes in boiling water until tender; drain and mash. Add cream cheese, butter, milk, salt and pepper; mix well. Stir in the green pepper, cheeses, chives and pimientos. Spread in a greased 13-in. x 9-in. x 2-in. baking dish. Bake, uncovered, at 350° for 50-60 minutes or until browned and heated through. **Yield:** 12-15 servings.

ROSY HOLIDAY PUNCH
Linda Ault, Newberry, Indiana

With its tangy juice and lovely blush color, this punch is fun to serve anytime. It's a refreshing beverage to go with a holiday meal or the season's sweet treats.

 1 bottle (32 ounces) cranberry juice
 1 can (12 ounces) frozen orange juice
  concentrate, thawed
 2 tablespoons sugar
 1/4 teaspoon ground allspice
 1 bottle (1 liter) ginger ale, chilled
Lemon and orange slices, optional

In a large container, combine cranberry juice, orange juice concentrate, sugar and allspice; mix well. Cover and chill at least 2 hours. Just before serving, add ginger ale; mix well. Garnish with lemon and orange slices if desired. **Yield:** 18-20 servings (about 1/2 cup each).

ROAST CHICKEN WITH CREOLE STUFFING
Ruth Bates, Temecula, California
(Pictured at right)

I've used this recipe ever since I roasted my first chicken. Our whole family looks forward to it. The combination of shrimp, sausage, ham, vegetables and seasonings makes the stuffing unique and delicious.

1-1/2 cups uncooked brown rice
 2 fresh Italian sausage links
 2 tablespoons cooking oil

 1 cup chopped onion
 5 garlic cloves, minced
 1/2 cup diced green pepper
 1/2 cup diced sweet red pepper
 1 can (14-1/2 ounces) diced tomatoes, undrained
 1 tablespoon lemon juice
 1 teaspoon dried basil
 1/2 teaspoon sugar
 1/2 teaspoon hot pepper sauce
 1/2 teaspoon chicken bouillon granules
 1/4 teaspoon chili powder
 1/4 teaspoon pepper
 1/8 teaspoon dried thyme
1-1/4 teaspoons salt, *divided*
 1 cup diced fully cooked ham
 1 cup frozen cooked small shrimp, thawed, optional
 3 tablespoons minced fresh parsley
 1 roasting chicken (5 to 6 pounds)
 1/2 teaspoon paprika
Dash pepper

In a large saucepan, cook rice according to package directions. Meanwhile, in a skillet, cook sausages in oil. Remove sausages, reserving drippings. When cool enough to handle, cut sausages in half lengthwise, then into 1/4-in. pieces; set aside. Saute onion, garlic and peppers in drippings until tender, about 4 minutes. Add the next nine ingredients and 1 teaspoon salt; cook and stir for 5 minutes. Add to the cooked rice. Stir in ham, shrimp if desired, parsley and sausage; mix lightly. Just before baking, stuff the chicken with about 3-1/2 cups stuffing. Place remaining stuffing in a greased 1-1/2-qt. baking dish; cover and refrigerate. Place chicken on a rack in a roasting pan; tie drumsticks together. Combine paprika, pepper and remaining salt; rub over chicken. Bake, uncovered, at 350° for 1-1/2 hours, basting every 30 minutes. Cover and bake 1-1/2 hours longer or until juices run clear. Bake additional stuffing for the last 40 minutes of baking time, uncovering during the last 10 minutes. **Yield:** 8-10 servings (8 cups stuffing).

Holiday Cookies

FROSTED CASHEW COOKIES
June Lindquist, Hammond, Wisconsin
(Pictured on page 32)

Some "dairy" merry snacking is guaranteed when you pass out these cashew-packed goodies! I found the recipe in a flyer promoting dairy products years ago. It's been this farm wife's standby ever since.

> 1/2 cup butter (no substitutes), softened
> 1 cup packed brown sugar
> 1 egg
> 1/2 teaspoon vanilla extract
> 2 cups all-purpose flour
> 3/4 teaspoon baking powder
> 3/4 teaspoon baking soda
> 1/4 teaspoon salt
> 1/3 cup sour cream
> 1-3/4 cups chopped cashews
> FROSTING:
> 1/2 cup butter (no substitutes)
> 3 tablespoons half-and-half cream
> 1/4 teaspoon vanilla extract
> 2 cups confectioners' sugar
> Cashew halves, optional

In a mixing bowl, cream butter and brown sugar. Beat in egg and vanilla. Combine dry ingredients; add alternately with sour cream to creamed mixture. Stir in cashews. Drop by tablespoonfuls onto greased baking sheets. Bake at 375° for 8-10 minutes or until lightly browned. Cool on a wire rack. For frosting, lightly brown butter in a small saucepan. Remove from the heat and cool slightly. Add cream and vanilla. Beat in confectioners' sugar until smooth and thick. Frost cookies; top each with a cashew half if desired. **Yield:** about 5 dozen.

CRISPY CHRISTMAS TREES
From the *Country Woman* Test Kitchen
(Pictured on page 33)

These holiday novelties will draw admiring comments wherever you serve them—a sprinkle of sugar supplies a Yuletide touch to each fanciful hand-shaped creation.

> 2 tablespoons butter (no substitutes)
> 2 cups pastel miniature marshmallows
> 3 cups crisp rice cereal
> 1/4 cup finely chopped pecans
> Green decorator's sugar
> Confectioners' sugar

In a heavy saucepan, melt butter. Stir in marshmallows; cook and stir over low heat until melted. Remove from the heat; stir in cereal and pecans. Let cool just enough to handle. With greased hands, shape into trees. (Work quickly as the cereal hardens quickly and becomes difficult to form.) Roll in green sugar. Place on a serving tray; dust with confectioners' sugar. **Yield:** about 1-1/2 dozen.

MERINGUE KISSES
Tami Henke, Lockport, Illinois
(Pictured on page 33)

There's a nice surprise of chocolate inside these frothy kisses. They're my husband's top choice each Christmas.

> 3 egg whites
> 1/4 teaspoon cream of tartar
> Pinch salt
> 1 cup sugar
> 1 teaspoon vanilla extract
> Red and green food coloring, optional
> 44 chocolate kisses

In a mixing bowl, beat egg whites until foamy. Sprinkle with cream of tartar and salt; beat until soft peaks form. Gradually add sugar and vanilla, beating until stiff peaks form, about 5-8 minutes. If desired, divide batter in half and fold in red and green food coloring. Drop by rounded tablespoonfuls 1-1/2 in. apart onto lightly greased baking sheets. Press a chocolate kiss into the center of each cookie and cover it with meringue using a knife. Bake at 275° for 30-35 minutes or until firm to the touch. Immediately remove to a wire rack to cool. Store in an airtight container. **Yield:** 44 cookies.

DATE SWIRL COOKIES
Linda Nilsen, Anoka, Minnesota
(Pictured on page 33)

Deliciously old-fashioned, these chewy treats have been a tradition in our family for 60 years. The recipe earned me a ribbon at the county fair and is a full-flavored winner anytime.

> 1-1/2 cups pitted dates, chopped
> 3/4 cup sugar, *divided*
> 1/3 cup water
> 1/4 cup chopped walnuts
> Pinch salt
> 1/2 cup butter (no substitutes), softened
> 1/2 cup packed brown sugar
> 1 egg
> 2 cups all-purpose flour
> 1/2 teaspoon baking soda
> 1/4 teaspoon salt

In a saucepan, combine dates, 1/4 cup sugar, water, nuts and salt. Cook over medium heat, stirring constantly, until thick, about 5 minutes. Set aside to cool. In a mixing bowl, beat butter, brown sugar, egg and remaining sugar. Combine flour, baking soda and salt; gradually stir into butter mixture. Chill for 30 minutes. Roll dough on a lightly floured surface to a 1/4-in.-thick rectangle. Spread with date mixture; roll up jelly-roll style, starting at a long end. Wrap with waxed paper. Chill for at least 4 hours. Remove waxed paper. Cut into 1/8-in. to 1/4-in. slices. Place 2 in. apart on greased baking sheets. Bake at 375° for 8 minutes. Cool on a wire rack. **Yield:** about 4 dozen.

CATHEDRAL COOKIES
Carol Shaffer, Cape Girardeau, Missouri
(Pictured on page 32)

Children love the colorful marshmallows in these festive confections, which look like stained glass when they're sliced. They practically light up the room from the serving platter at our holiday parties.

    1 cup (6 ounces) semisweet chocolate chips
    2 tablespoons butter (no substitutes)
    1 egg, beaten
    3 cups pastel miniature marshmallows
1/2 cup chopped pecans *or* walnuts
    1 cup flaked coconut

In a heavy saucepan, melt chocolate chips and butter over low heat, stirring occasionally. Stir a small amount into the egg, then return all to pan. Cook and stir over low heat for 2 minutes. Pour into a bowl; let cool for 15 minutes. Gently stir in marshmallows and nuts. Chill for 30 minutes. Turn onto a sheet of waxed paper. Form into a roll about 1-1/2 in. in diameter. Gently roll onto another sheet of waxed paper sprinkled with coconut. Using the waxed paper, cover the outside of the roll with the coconut. Wrap roll tightly, twisting ends to seal. Freeze for 4 hours or overnight. Remove waxed paper. Cut into 1/4-in. slices. Store in an airtight container in the refrigerator. **Yield:** about 5 dozen.

HOLIDAY CHEESECAKE BARS
Kathy Dorman, Snover, Michigan
(Pictured on pages 32 and 33)

Christmas officially arrives at our house when I make these melt-in-your-mouth bars. Red and green maraschino cherries add a jolly finish to each light and creamy morsel.

    2 cups all-purpose flour
2/3 cup packed brown sugar
2/3 cup cold butter (no substitutes)
    1 cup chopped walnuts
FILLING:
    2 packages (8 ounces *each*) cream cheese, softened
1/2 cup sugar
    2 eggs
1/4 cup milk
    2 tablespoons lemon juice
    1 teaspoon vanilla extract
Sliced red and green maraschino cherries, optional

In a bowl, combine flour and brown sugar; cut in butter until mixture resembles coarse crumbs. Stir in walnuts. Reserve 1 cup. Press remaining crumbs onto the bottom of an ungreased 13-in. x 9-in. x 2-in. baking pan. Bake at 350° for 12 minutes. Meanwhile, in a mixing bowl, beat cream cheese and sugar until light and fluffy. Add eggs, one at a time, beating well after each addition. Beat in milk, lemon juice and vanilla; pour over crust. Sprinkle with reserved crumbs. Bake 25-30 minutes longer or until edges are lightly browned and filling is almost set. Cool in pan on a wire rack. Cut into squares. Garnish with cherries if desired. Store in the refrigerator. **Yield:** 2 dozen.

CHRISTMAS CUTOUTS
Shirley Kidd, New London, Minnesota
(Pictured on page 32)

Making and decorating these tender sugar cookies left a lasting impression on our four children. Now that they're grown, they've all asked for my recipe so they can bake them with their own children.

    1 cup butter (no substitutes), softened
1-1/2 cups confectioners' sugar
    1 egg
    1 teaspoon vanilla extract
1/2 teaspoon almond extract
2-1/2 cups all-purpose flour
    1 teaspoon baking soda
    1 teaspoon cream of tartar
FROSTING:
    4 cups confectioners' sugar
    3 tablespoons butter (no substitutes), softened
    1 teaspoon vanilla extract
2-1/2 to 3 tablespoons milk
Liquid *or* paste food coloring, optional

In a mixing bowl, cream butter and sugar. Add egg and extracts. Combine flour, baking soda and cream of tartar; gradually add to the creamed mixture and mix well. Chill for 2-3 hours. On a lightly floured surface, roll dough to 1/8-in. thickness. Cut into desired shapes. Place on ungreased baking sheets. Bake at 375° for 7-8 minutes or until edges begin to brown. Cool on a wire rack. For frosting, beat sugar, butter and vanilla in a mixing bowl. Gradually stir in milk until smooth and thick; add food coloring if desired. Frost cookies. **Yield:** 5 dozen (2-inch cookies).

CHOCOLATE CHIP PUMPKIN COOKIES
Heidi Harrington, Steuben, Maine

As a fun alternative to pumpkin pie, I often make these easy drop cookies. The chocolate chips and harvest-fresh goodness make them special enough for a holiday dessert.

    4 cups all-purpose flour
    2 cups sugar
    2 teaspoons ground cinnamon
    2 teaspoons baking soda
    1 teaspoon salt
    1 can (16 ounces) solid-pack pumpkin
    1 cup vegetable oil
    2 eggs
    2 tablespoons milk
    2 teaspoons vanilla extract
    2 cups (12 ounces) semisweet chocolate chips
    1 cup chopped walnuts

In a mixing bowl, combine flour, sugar, cinnamon, baking soda and salt. Add pumpkin, oil, eggs, milk and vanilla; beat on medium speed until well mixed. Stir in chocolate chips and nuts. Drop by tablespoonfuls onto greased baking sheets. Bake at 375° for 13-14 minutes or until edges just begin to brown. Cool for 2 minutes; remove to a wire rack to cool completely. **Yield:** about 7 dozen.

COOKIE COLLAGE. Starting clockwise from bottom right: Crispy Christmas Trees (p. 30), Christmas Cutouts (p. 31), Frosted Cashew Cookies (p. 30), Cathedral Cookies (p. 31), Meringue Kisses (p. 30), Date Swirl Cookies (p. 30) and Holiday Cheesecake Bars, center (p. 31).

SIMPLE SESAMES
Jennifer Lynn, Kamiah, Idaho

My kitchen counter is covered with these crispy crowd-pleasers at Christmastime. I make them for friends and family. I also add them to care packages our church delivers to area senior citizens.

　　1 cup butter (no substitutes), softened
　　3/4 cup sugar
1-1/2 cups all-purpose flour
　　1 cup flaked coconut
　　1/2 cup sesame seeds
　　1/4 cup finely chopped almonds

In a mixing bowl, cream butter and sugar. Add flour; mix just until combined. Stir in coconut, sesame seeds and almonds. Chill for 15 minutes. Divide dough in half. Shape each half into a 2-in.-diameter roll. Wrap each roll in waxed paper, twisting ends to seal. Refrigerate for 2 hours or overnight. Remove waxed paper. Cut into 1/4-in. slices; place on ungreased baking sheets. Bake at 300° for 20-25 minutes or until lightly browned. Cool for 2 minutes; remove to a wire rack to cool completely. **Yield:** about 3-1/2 dozen.

COCONUT CHERRY BARS
Cynthia Lovell, Farmington, Maine

I enjoy whipping up batches of these by the dozens. Then I fill the decorative tins I collect all year long with the luscious bars and give them as oven-fresh Christmas presents. Everyone loves them!

　　2 cups all-purpose flour
　　1/3 cup sugar
　　3/4 cup cold butter (no substitutes)
FILLING:
　　1 cup packed brown sugar
　　1/3 cup all-purpose flour
1-1/2 teaspoons baking powder
　　1/2 teaspoon salt
　　2 eggs
　　1 teaspoon vanilla extract
　　1 jar (10 ounces) red *or* green maraschino cherries
　　1/2 cup chopped walnuts
FROSTING:
　　2 tablespoons butter (no substitutes), softened
2-1/2 cups confectioners' sugar
　　1 cup flaked coconut

Combine flour and sugar; cut in butter until crumbly. Press into an ungreased 13-in. x 9-in. x 2-in. baking pan. Bake at 350° for 15-18 minutes or until lightly browned. For filling, combine brown sugar, flour, baking powder and salt; mix in eggs and vanilla. Drain cherries, reserving juice. Chop cherries; fold into batter along with walnuts. Pour over crust. Bake 20-25 minutes longer or until a toothpick inserted near the center comes out clean. Cool. For frosting, beat butter and sugar in a mixing bowl. Gradually stir in 3-4 tablespoons reserved cherry juice until frosting reaches desired spreading consistency. Frost bars; sprinkle with coconut. **Yield:** 3 dozen.

LEMON COCONUT BARS
Doris Jean Armstrong, Santa Fe, New Mexico

When I pull these cookies from the oven, everyone gathers to catch a citrusy whiff. The lemony filling, with its chewy coconut texture, squeezes a welcome hint of sunshine into each satisfying bite.

　　1/2 cup butter (no substitutes), softened
　　1 cup sugar
　　1 egg
　　1/4 cup molasses
2-1/4 cups all-purpose flour
　　1 teaspoon cinnamon
　　1/2 teaspoon baking soda
　　1/4 teaspoon salt
FILLING:
　　1/2 cup sugar
　　1/4 cup lemon juice
　　1 tablespoon grated lemon peel
　　1 tablespoon butter (no substitutes)
　　2 eggs
　　1/8 teaspoon salt
　　1 cup flaked coconut

In a mixing bowl, cream butter and sugar. Beat in egg and molasses. Combine flour, cinnamon, baking soda and salt; gradually add to creamed mixture and mix well. Refrigerate for 2 hours or overnight. For filling, in a saucepan, combine sugar, lemon juice, peel, butter, eggs and salt. Cook and stir over low heat until thickened, about 10 minutes. Remove from the heat; stir in coconut. Cool slightly; chill. Divide dough into fourths. Roll each portion into a 15-in. x 3-1/2-in. rectangle. Spread 1/4 cup filling off-center down each rectangle. Bring long edges together over filling; seal edges. Cut into 1-1/2-in. bars; place on ungreased baking sheets. Bake at 350° for 12-15 minutes or until edges are lightly browned. Cool for 2 minutes; remove to a wire rack to cool completely. **Yield:** about 3-1/2 dozen.

FRUITCAKE SQUARES
Nora Seaton, McLean, Virginia

My family prefers these scrumptious squares to the larger, more traditional fruitcake. Since they're so quick and simple to make, I always include several batches in my annual holiday baking spree.

　　6 tablespoons butter (no substitutes), melted
　　4 cups vanilla wafer crumbs
　　1 cup pecan halves
　　3/4 cup chopped dates
　　3/4 cup chopped mixed candied fruit
　　1/2 cup chopped candied pineapple
　　1 can (14 ounces) sweetened condensed milk
　　1 teaspoon vanilla extract

Pour butter into a 15-in. x 10-in. x 1-in. baking pan. Sprinkle with wafer crumbs. Arrange pecans and fruit over crumbs; press down gently. Combine milk and vanilla; pour evenly over fruit. Bake at 350° for 20-25 minutes or until lightly browned. Cool on a wire rack. **Yield:** about 3 dozen.

GINGERBREAD COOKIES WITH BUTTERCREAM ICING

Ann Scherzer, Anacortes, Washington
(Pictured above)

These holiday-spiced cookies are the first ones I make in December. The recipe came from my mother-in-law. If you like, tint the buttery icing a cheery pink or green and pipe it on with a decorating tip.

   2/3 cup shortening
   1 cup sugar
   1 egg
1/4 cup molasses
   2 cups all-purpose flour
   1 teaspoon baking soda
   1 teaspoon salt
   1 teaspoon *each* ground cinnamon, cloves and ginger

ICING:
   3 cups confectioners' sugar
1/3 cup butter (no substitutes), softened
   1 teaspoon vanilla extract
1/4 teaspoon lemon extract
1/4 teaspoon butter flavoring
   3 to 4 tablespoons milk

In a mixing bowl, cream shortening and sugar. Beat in egg and molasses. Combine flour, baking soda, salt and spices; gradually add to the creamed mixture and mix well. Refrigerate for 2 hours or overnight. On a lightly floured surface, roll dough to 1/4-in. thickness. Cut into desired shapes. Place on ungreased baking sheets. Bake at 350° for 8-10 minutes or until edges begin to brown. Cool on a wire rack. For icing, beat sugar, butter and flavorings in a mixing bowl. Gradually stir in milk until smooth and thick. Frost cookies. **Yield:** about 3-1/2 dozen (2-1/2-inch cookies).

COLORFUL CONFECTIONS! Clockwise, starting from top right: Old-Time Butter Crunch Candy (p. 37), Homemade Marshmallows (p. 38), Chocolate Nut Fudge Rolls (p. 37), Hard Candy (p. 38), Butter Mints (p. 37) and Chocolate-Covered Cherries (p. 37).

Seasonal Sweets

OLD-TIME BUTTER CRUNCH CANDY
Mildred Duffy, Bella Vista, Arkansas
(Pictured on page 36)

Both my children and my grandchildren say the season wouldn't be the same without the big tray of candies and cookies I prepare. This one's a popular part of that collection. We love the nutty pieces draped in chocolate.

    1 cup butter (no substitutes)
1-1/4 cups sugar
    2 tablespoons light corn syrup
    2 tablespoons water
    2 cups finely chopped toasted almonds
    8 milk chocolate candy bars (1.55 ounces *each*)

Line a 13-in. x 9-in. x 2-in. baking pan with foil; set aside. Using part of the butter, grease the sides of a large heavy saucepan. Add remaining butter to saucepan; melt over low heat. Add sugar, corn syrup and water. Cook and stir over medium heat until a candy thermometer reads 300° (hard-crack stage). Remove from the heat and stir in almonds. Quickly pour into the prepared pan, spreading to cover bottom of pan. Cool completely. Carefully invert pan to remove candy in one piece; remove foil. Melt half of the chocolate in a double boiler or microwave-safe bowl; spread over top of candy. Let cool. Turn candy over and repeat with remaining chocolate; cool. Break into 2-in. pieces. Store in an airtight container. **Yield:** about 2 pounds.

CHOCOLATE-COVERED CHERRIES
Lori O'Brien, Milbank, South Dakota
(Pictured on page 36)

Each year, I have to plan on producing even more of these simple-to-make candies—they're the ones my husband likes best, and they're the first to disappear.

    1/2 cup butter *or* margarine, softened
    2 cups marshmallow creme
Pinch salt
    1 teaspoon almond extract
    4 cups confectioners' sugar
    1 jar (16 ounces) maraschino cherries, well
        drained
    2 cups (12 ounces) semisweet chocolate chips
    2 tablespoons shortening

In a mixing bowl, cream butter. Add marshmallow creme, salt, extract and sugar; mix well. Knead into a large ball; chill for 1 hour. Roll into 1-in. balls and flatten into 2-in. circles. Wrap circles around cherries and carefully shape into balls. Place on a waxed paper-lined baking sheet. Cover loosely; refrigerate for 4 hours or overnight. Melt chocolate chips and shortening in a double boiler or microwave-safe bowl. Dip cherries into chocolate; place on waxed paper to harden. Refrigerate in a covered container 1-2 weeks before serving. **Yield:** about 4-1/2 dozen.

BUTTER MINTS
Bev Schloneger, Dalton, Ohio
(Pictured on page 36)

These creamy mints are smooth as silk and melt in your mouth! As a wife and mother of three youngsters, I treasure treats like these that come together quickly but taste terrific.

    1/2 cup butter (no substitutes), softened
    1 package (1 pound) confectioners' sugar
    1 tablespoon half-and-half cream *or* milk
    1 teaspoon vanilla extract
    1/4 teaspoon peppermint extract
Red and green paste *or* liquid food coloring, optional

In a mixing bowl, cream the butter. Gradually add sugar, cream and extracts; beat on medium speed for 3-4 minutes. If desired, divide dough into portions and knead in food coloring. Form into balls by teaspoonfuls; flatten into patties, or roll between two pieces of waxed paper to 1/8-in. thickness and cut into desired shapes. Cover and refrigerate for several hours or overnight. Store in the refrigerator. **Yield:** about 8 dozen.

CHOCOLATE NUT FUDGE ROLLS
Connie Korbel, Lakeport, California
(Pictured on page 36)

The recipe for these rich chocolaty nut rolls comes from a handwritten cookbook full of memorable holiday treats—my mother compiled it for me the last Christmas I lived at home.

    2 tablespoons butter *or* margarine
    1 square (1 ounce) unsweetened chocolate
    3 cups sugar
    1 cup milk
    1/4 cup honey
    1/8 teaspoon salt
    1 teaspoon vinegar
    1 teaspoon vanilla extract
    2 cups (12 ounces) semisweet chocolate chips
    1 tablespoon shortening
    3 cups chopped walnuts

In a large heavy saucepan, melt butter and chocolate over low heat. Add sugar, milk, honey and salt. Bring to a boil over medium heat, stirring occasionally. Cover and continue to boil for 2 minutes. Uncover and cook, without stirring, until a candy thermometer reads 240° (soft-ball stage). Remove from the heat; stir in vinegar. Let cool to 110°. Add vanilla; beat vigorously by hand until mixture thickens and loses its gloss, about 8-10 minutes. Turn onto a buttered baking sheet. Let stand until cool enough to handle. Knead for 2-3 minutes. Shape into 4-in. x 1-1/2-in. rolls. Place on waxed paper-lined baking sheets; chill for 3-4 hours. Melt chocolate chips and shortening in a double boiler or microwave-safe bowl. Dip rolls in chocolate; roll in nuts. Place on waxed paper-lined baking sheets and chill until firm. Cut into 1/4-in. slices. **Yield:** about 2-1/4 pounds.

HARD CANDY
Virginia Sue Barlow, Farmer City, Illinois
(Pictured on page 36)

Every evening for a week in December, my husband and I mix up several batches of this soothing candy. When we finish, we have all our favorite flavors and a rainbow of colors. The pieces look lovely in a clear candy dish or jar.

    5 to 6 cups confectioners' sugar
    2 cups sugar
  3/4 cup light corn syrup
  1/2 cup water
    1 to 2 teaspoons anise, lemon *or* orange extract
Red, yellow *or* orange liquid food coloring, optional

Fill a 15-in. x 10-in. x 1-in. baking pan with confectioners' sugar to a depth of 1/2 in. Using the handle of a wooden spoon, make a continuous curved-line indentation in the sugar; set pan aside. In a large heavy saucepan, combine sugar, corn syrup and water. Bring to a boil over medium heat, stirring occasionally. Cover and continue cooking for 3 minutes to dissolve any sugar crystals. Uncover and cook on medium-high heat, without stirring, until a candy thermometer reads 300° (hard-crack stage). Remove from the heat; stir in extract and food coloring if desired (keep face away from mixture because aroma is very strong). Carefully pour into a glass measuring cup. Working quickly, pour into prepared indentation in pan. Cover candy with confectioners' sugar. When candy is cool enough to handle, cut into pieces with a scissors. Store in a covered container. **Yield:** 3/4 pound.

HOMEMADE MARSHMALLOWS
Nancy Shields, Hillsdale, Michigan
(Pictured on page 36)

My husband Dale's grandmother fixed these fluffy marshmallows only for special occasions. Since she had no electric mixer, beating the ingredients by hand for 30 minutes was a labor of love. Now, Dale makes them. They're delicious!

    2 cups cold water, *divided*
    4 envelopes unflavored gelatin
    4 cups sugar
  1/8 teaspoon salt
    2 teaspoons vanilla extract
Confectioners' sugar
Toasted flaked coconut *or* ground pecans, optional

In a large mixing bowl, combine 3/4 cup of water and gelatin; set aside. In a large heavy saucepan over medium heat, combine sugar, salt and remaining water. Bring to a boil, stirring occasionally. Cover and continue cooking for 3 minutes to dissolve any sugar crystals. Uncover and cook on medium-high heat, without stirring, until a candy thermometer reads 270° (soft-crack stage). Remove from the heat and gradually add to gelatin. Beat on low speed for 3 minutes. Add vanilla; beat on medium for 10 minutes. Spread mixture into a 13-in. x 9-in. x 2-in. pan sprinkled with confectioners' sugar. Cover and cool at room temperature for 6 hours or overnight. Cut into 1-in. squares; roll in coconut or nuts if desired. Store in airtight containers in a cool dry place. **Yield:** about 8 dozen.

CRUNCHY PEANUT CANDY
Vicki Jensen, Spencer, Iowa

I got this recipe from a man I worked with 10 years ago and have made it for Christmas ever since. The chunky bites are fun to fix—and fun to eat!

    1 package (18 ounces) white confectionery coating*
    1 cup chunky peanut butter
    2 cups dry roasted peanuts
    2 cups miniature marshmallows
    3 cups crisp rice cereal

In a large roasting pan or Dutch oven, heat confectionery coating in a 200° oven for 15 minutes or until melted. Stir in peanut butter. Fold in remaining ingredients. Drop by tablespoonfuls onto waxed paper. Chill until set. **Yield:** 7 dozen. ***Editor's Note:** Confectionery coating is found in the baking section of most grocery stores. It is sometimes labeled "almond bark" or "candy coating" and is sold in bulk packages of 1 to 1-1/2 pounds.

CHOCOLATE PEPPERMINT CANDIES
Jeanne Fry, Greensburg, Indiana

The cool mint filling in these patties makes them especially delicious. Friends often request that I bring them to parties.

  3/4 cup sweetened condensed milk
1-1/2 teaspoons peppermint extract
    4 to 4-1/2 cups confectioners' sugar
    3 cups (18 ounces) semisweet chocolate chips
    2 teaspoons shortening

In a bowl, combine milk and extract. Stir in 3-1/2 to 4 cups confectioners' sugar to form a stiff dough. Turn onto a surface sprinkled lightly with confectioners' sugar. Knead in enough remaining sugar to form a dough that is very stiff and no longer sticky. Shape into 1-in. balls. Place on a waxed paper-lined baking sheet. Flatten into 1-1/2-in. circles. Let dry 1 hour. Turn and let dry 1 hour longer. Melt chocolate chips and shortening in a double boiler or microwave-safe bowl; cool slightly. Dip patties in chocolate mixture and place on waxed paper to harden. **Yield:** 3 dozen.

CHOCOLATE NUT CANDIES
Mary Parker, Copperas Cove, Texas

I've been making these yummy candies for many years. With their three rich gooey layers, a little goes a long way. One batch is enough to please a crowd.

    3 cups (18 ounces) semisweet chocolate chips
    2 cups creamy peanut butter
    1 cup butter *or* margarine
  1/2 cup evaporated milk
  1/4 cup instant vanilla pudding mix
    1 teaspoon vanilla extract

2 pounds confectioners' sugar
3 cups salted peanuts

In a heavy saucepan over low heat, melt chocolate chips and peanut butter, stirring frequently. Pour half into a greased 15-in. x 10-in. x 1-in. baking pan; chill. Set remaining chocolate mixture aside. In another saucepan, bring butter, milk and pudding mix to a boil; boil for 1 minute, stirring constantly. Remove from the heat; pour into a large bowl; add vanilla. Gradually stir in sugar. Spread over chocolate layer in baking pan; chill. Add peanuts to reserved chocolate mixture; spread over filling. Chill. Cut into 1-in. x 1/2-in. pieces. **Yield:** 25 dozen.

BUTTERSCOTCH TAFFY
Teri Lindquist, Wildwood, Illinois

It's a good thing that this recipe isn't a lot of fuss—the soft tempting taffy goes so fast I sometimes don't even get to wrap the pieces!

  1/2 cup butter *or* margarine
   48 large marshmallows
    1 tablespoon water
  1/2 teaspoon salt
    2 cups (12 ounces) butterscotch chips

In a heavy saucepan, combine butter, marshmallows, water and salt; cook and stir over low heat until smooth. Add chips; stir until melted. Pour into a buttered 8-in. square baking pan; cool. Cut into 1-in. squares. Wrap individually in waxed paper; twist ends. **Yield:** about 5 dozen.

CRANBERRY GUMDROPS
Elaine Thu, Graettinger, Iowa

This unique treat combines two holiday favorites—the tangy flavor of cranberry and a sweet chewy candy. I've made them for years. They're popular with all ages.

    2 envelopes unflavored gelatin
  1/2 cup cold water
    1 can (16 ounces) jellied cranberry sauce
    2 cups sugar, *divided*
    3 packages (3 ounces *each*) raspberry gelatin
Additional sugar, optional

In a saucepan, sprinkle unflavored gelatin over water; let stand for 2 minutes to soften. Add cranberry sauce and 1 cup of sugar; cook over low heat until sauce is melted and sugar is dissolved, about 10 minutes. Whisk until smooth. Remove from the heat and add raspberry gelatin; stir until completely dissolved, about 3 minutes. Pour into an 8-in. square baking pan coated with nonstick cooking spray. Cover and let stand at room temperature for 12 hours or overnight (do not refrigerate). Cut into 1-in. squares; roll in remaining sugar. Place on baking sheets; let stand at room temperature for 3 hours. Turn pieces over and let stand 3 hours longer. Roll in additional sugar if desired. Store in an airtight container at room temperature. **Yield:** about 5 dozen.

PENUCHE
Rosemarie Anderson, Great Valley, New York

My mom used to make this brown sugar fudge every year during the holidays, both for our family and to give as gifts. It has such wonderful old-fashioned flavor. We still savor the tradition.

    2 cups packed brown sugar
    1 cup sugar
    1 cup half-and-half cream
    2 tablespoons light corn syrup
    1 teaspoon lemon juice
Pinch salt
    2 tablespoons butter (no substitutes)
    1 teaspoon vanilla extract
  1/2 cup chopped pecans

In a large heavy saucepan, combine sugars, cream, corn syrup, lemon juice and salt. Bring to a boil over medium heat, stirring occasionally. Cook, without stirring, until a candy thermometer reads 238° (soft-ball stage). Hold at soft-ball stage for 5-6 minutes. Remove from the heat. Add butter; do not stir. Cool to 110°. Stir in vanilla; beat vigorously by hand until mixture is very thick and slightly lighter in color, about 20 minutes. Quickly stir in pecans, then pour into a greased 8-in. square pan. Cool. Cut into 1-in. squares. **Yield:** 1-3/4 pounds.

OLD-FASHIONED CARAMELS
Jan Batman, Oskaloosa, Iowa

Before I was married, my future father-in-law would fix these creamy caramels at Christmas and send me some. The recipe has been in my husband's family for decades...so, when we got married, I learned to make them, too.

    2 cups sugar
1-3/4 cups light corn syrup
    1 cup butter *or* margarine
    2 cups half-and-half cream
    1 teaspoon vanilla extract
    1 cup chopped pecans, optional

Line an 11-in. x 7-in. x 2-in. pan with foil; butter the foil and set aside. In a large heavy saucepan over medium heat, combine sugar, corn syrup and butter. Bring to a boil, stirring constantly; boil gently for 4 minutes without stirring. Remove from the heat and stir in cream. Reduce heat to medium-low and cook until a candy thermometer reads 238° (soft-ball stage), stirring constantly. Remove from the heat; stir in vanilla and pecans if desired. Pour into prepared pan; cool. Remove from pan and cut into 1-in. squares. Wrap individually in waxed paper; twist ends. **Yield:** about 6 dozen.

● It's a good idea to test your candy thermometer before each use. Fill a 2-cup glass measuring cup with water; bring to a boil. Insert the thermometer. It should read 212°. If it doesn't, adjust your recipe temperature up or down accordingly.

Festive Desserts

CANDY CANE CHEESECAKE
Gwen Koob-Roach, Saskatoon, Saskatchewan
(Pictured on page 41)

This pepperminty cheesecake says "Christmas" at first sight and first bite. The recipe earned me a dairy producer's scholarship. Now, it regularly wins compliments at seasonal parties and teas.

1-1/2 cups chocolate wafer crumbs
  1/3 cup butter *or* margarine, melted
    2 tablespoons sugar
FILLING:
    3 packages (8 ounces *each*) cream cheese, softened
  3/4 cup sugar
    3 tablespoons all-purpose flour
    4 eggs
    1 cup (8 ounces) sour cream
    2 tablespoons vanilla baking chips
  1/2 to 3/4 teaspoon peppermint extract
Red liquid *or* paste food coloring
Crushed peppermint candy and whipped topping, optional

Combine the first three ingredients; press onto the bottom of a 9-in. springform pan. Chill. In a mixing bowl, beat cream cheese and sugar until smooth; add flour and mix well. Add the eggs, one at a time, beating just until blended. Stir in sour cream. Set aside. In a small saucepan over low heat, melt vanilla chips. Remove from the heat. Add 1/4 cup cream cheese mixture, extract and a few drops of food coloring; mix well. Pour half of the remaining cream cheese mixture over crust. Top with half of the peppermint mixture; swirl with a knife. Repeat layers. Bake at 450° for 10 minutes. Reduce heat to 250°; bake 40-50 minutes longer or until the center is almost set. Cool on a wire rack for 1 hour. Chill for at least 3 hours. Just before serving, remove sides of pan. Garnish with crushed candy and whipped topping if desired. **Yield:** 12-16 servings.

BUTTERSCOTCH PUMPKIN PUFFS
Michelle Smith, Running Springs, California
(Pictured on page 41)

Yummy things come in these little pudding-rich "packages". The puffs can be made and frozen in advance, then filled before serving for a time-saving Yuletide dessert.

    2 packages (3.4 ounces *each*) instant butterscotch pudding mix
    1 can (12 ounces) evaporated milk
  1/2 teaspoon ground cinnamon
  1/4 teaspoon ground ginger
    1 cup canned *or* cooked pumpkin
    1 cup whipped topping, optional
CREAM PUFFS:
1-1/2 cups water
  3/4 cup butter *or* margarine
  1/2 teaspoon salt

1-1/2 cups all-purpose flour
    6 eggs
  1/3 cup confectioners' sugar
  1/3 cup semisweet chocolate chips, melted

In a mixing bowl, combine pudding mix, milk and spices; beat on medium speed for 30 seconds. Blend in pumpkin and whipped topping if desired. Refrigerate for 1 hour or overnight. In a medium saucepan, combine water, butter and salt; bring to a boil. Reduce heat to low; add flour all at once and stir until a smooth ball forms. Remove from the heat; add eggs, one at a time, beating well after each addition with an electric mixer. Continue beating until mixture is smooth and shiny. Drop by tablespoonfuls 2 in. apart onto greased baking sheets. Bake at 400° for 10 minutes. Reduce heat to 350°; bake 25 minutes longer or until golden brown. Remove from the oven; turn oven off. Cut a slit halfway through each puff and return to the oven for 30 minutes with the oven door open. Cool on a wire rack. Just before serving, spoon about 1 tablespoon filling into each puff. Dust with confectioners' sugar and drizzle with melted chocolate. **Yield:** 5 dozen.

PECAN MACADAMIA PIE
Anne Simboli, Farmville, Virginia
(Pictured on page 41)

It's bound to be a blue-ribbon Christmas when I serve this rich, nutty pie—it was a prize-winner at our county fair. Even my husband, who can take or leave sweets, can't resist it!

    1 cup all-purpose flour
    2 tablespoons sugar
  1/2 teaspoon salt
  1/4 cup shortening
    3 to 4 tablespoons cold water
FILLING:
    3 eggs
  1/2 cup sugar
4-1/2 teaspoons all-purpose flour
  1/4 teaspoon salt
    1 cup light corn syrup
    1 tablespoon butter *or* margarine, melted and cooled
    1 teaspoon vanilla extract
    1 cup coarsely chopped pecans
  3/4 cup coarsely chopped macadamia nuts

In a bowl, combine flour, sugar and salt; cut in shortening until crumbly. Gradually add cold water, tossing with a fork until dough begins to cling together. Form into a ball. On a lightly floured surface, roll dough to a 10-in. circle. Place in a 9-in. pie plate and set aside. For filling, beat eggs until blended but not frothy. Add sugar, flour, salt and corn syrup; mix well. Add butter and vanilla; mix just until blended. Stir in nuts. Pour into crust. Place in a 350° oven and immediately reduce heat to 325°. Bake for 55-60 minutes or until center is set. Cool on a wire rack. Store in the refrigerator. **Yield:** 8-10 servings.

DELIGHTFUL DESSERTS! Clockwise from top left: Candy Cane Cheesecake (p. 40), Butterscotch Pumpkin Puffs (p. 40), Cherry Cheese Cupcakes (p. 42) and Pecan Macadamia Pie (p. 40).

CHERRY CHEESE CUPCAKES
Leanne Beagley, Rochester, New York
(Pictured on page 41)

Our church Christmas party always includes these pretty cupcakes as my home-baked contribution. The holidays were the sweet inspiration for their cheery garnish of cherries and mint leaves.

      3 packages (8 ounces *each*) cream cheese, softened
1-1/2 cups sugar, *divided*
1-1/2 teaspoons vanilla extract, *divided*
      5 eggs
      1 cup (8 ounces) sour cream
1-1/2 cups cherry pie filling
Mint leaves

In a mixing bowl, combine cream cheese, 1 cup sugar and 1 teaspoon vanilla; beat until smooth. Add eggs, one at a time, beating well after each addition. Spoon into foil-lined muffin cups. Bake at 300° for 25-30 minutes or until set. Cool 5 minutes. In a small bowl, combine sour cream and the remaining sugar and vanilla until smooth. Spoon onto cupcakes. Return to the oven for 6-8 minutes or until set. Cool completely. Top with pie filling. Garnish with mint leaves. Chill. **Yield:** 22-24 servings.

EGGNOG TRIFLE
Cynthia Butt, Winnipeg, Manitoba

This classic Christmas dessert is too delicious to have just once a year. So our family serves it for birthdays…and whatever other occasion we can think of!

3/4 cup cold milk
      1 package (3.4 ounces) instant vanilla pudding mix
      2 cups eggnog*
1/2 teaspoon almond extract
1-1/2 cups whipping cream, whipped, *divided*
      1 loaf (10 ounces) angel food *or* sponge cake
      1 cup raspberry jam *or* preserves
      2 tablespoons confectioners' sugar
1/2 teaspoon vanilla extract
Maraschino cherry halves

In a mixing bowl, beat milk and pudding mix until blended. Gradually add eggnog; mix well. Fold in extract and 1 cup of whipped cream; set aside. Slice cake into 1/2-in. pieces; place a fourth in a 2-qt. serving bowl. Top with 1/3 cup jam. Spoon 1 cup of eggnog mixture over all. Repeat two more layers of cake, jam and eggnog mixture. Top with remaining cake and eggnog mixture. Cover and chill for at least 2 hours. Fold sugar and vanilla into remaining whipped cream; spoon on top of trifle. Garnish with cherries. **Yield:** 8-10 servings. ***Editor's Note:** This recipe was tested with commercially prepared eggnog.

TRIPLE CHOCOLATE DELIGHT
Mrs. Edwin Hill, Santa Barbara, California

A fitting finale for any special occasion, this fudgy cake has three luscious layers for chocolate lovers to sink their forks into.

      1 cup butter *or* margarine, softened, *divided*
      2 cups sugar
      4 eggs
      5 Milky Way candy bars (2.15 ounces *each*)
1-1/4 cups buttermilk
2-1/2 cups all-purpose flour
      1/2 teaspoon baking soda
      1/4 teaspoon salt
      1 cup chopped walnuts
FROSTING:
      1/2 cup butter *or* margarine, *divided*
2-1/2 cups sugar
      1 cup evaporated milk
      1 jar (7 ounces) marshmallow creme
      1 cup (6 ounces) semisweet chocolate chips
Chopped walnuts, optional

In a large mixing bowl, cream 1/2 cup butter and sugar. Add eggs, one at a time, beating well after each addition. In a heavy saucepan, stir candy bars and remaining butter over low heat until melted. Remove from the heat; stir in buttermilk. Combine flour, baking soda and salt; add alternately with buttermilk mixture to creamed mixture. Fold in nuts. Pour into three greased and floured 8-in. round cake pans. Bake at 350° for 30-40 minutes or until a toothpick inserted near the center comes out clean. Cool in pans on a rack for 10 minutes; remove from pans to cool completely. For frosting, lightly grease the sides of a medium saucepan with part of the butter. Set remaining butter aside. Combine sugar and milk in the pan; cook over medium heat, stirring occasionally, until mixture comes to a rolling boil. Boil until a candy thermometer reads 234° (soft-ball stage). Remove from the heat; stir in marshmallow creme, chips and remaining butter. Transfer to a mixing bowl and cool to 110°. Beat on medium speed until smooth, about 5-7 minutes. Immediately frost cooled cake. Sprinkle with walnuts if desired. **Yield:** 12 servings.

BANBURY TARTS
From the *Country Woman* Test Kitchen

Deliciously old-fashioned, these tempting tarts are a "must" for Santa's Christmas Eve cookie plate.

      1 cup chopped raisins
      1 cup sugar
      1/4 cup graham cracker crumbs
      1 egg
      2 tablespoons lemon juice
      2 teaspoons grated lemon peel
      1/4 cup finely chopped walnuts, optional
Pastry for two double-crust pies (9 inches)
      1 cup confectioners' sugar
      4 teaspoons milk

In a bowl, combine the first six ingredients. Stir in walnuts if desired. Roll out pastry to 1/8-in. thickness; cut into 48 3-in. circles; moisten edges with water. Put 1-1/2 teaspoons filling on half of each circle. Fold other half over the filling; press edges together with a fork to seal. Cut a slit in top of each tart. Place on a lightly greased baking sheet. Bake at 375° for 13-15 minutes or until lightly browned. Remove to wire racks to cool. Combine sugar and milk; drizzle over cooled tarts. **Yield:** 4 dozen.

Gifts from the Kitchen

and ribbons, you can tuck them into stockings, tie them onto gifts or slip them inside a glass jar.

> 2 packages (14 ounces *each*) caramels
> 2 packages (10 ounces *each*) pretzel rods
> 3 cups chopped toasted almonds
> 1 pound white confectionery coating*
> 1 pound dark chocolate confectionery coating*

Melt caramels in the top of a double boiler or microwave-safe bowl. Pour into an ungreased 8-in. square pan or a tall glass. Leaving 1 in. of space on the end you are holding, roll or dip pretzels in caramel. Allow excess to drip off. Roll in almonds. Place on waxed paper-lined baking sheets and allow to harden. Melt white confectionery coating in a double boiler or microwave-safe bowl. Repeat dipping procedure with half of the caramel-coated pretzels. Return to baking sheets to harden. Repeat with dark chocolate coating and remaining pretzels. Store in an airtight container, or wrap in plastic wrap and tie with a colorful ribbon for gift-giving. **Yield:** about 4 dozen.
*Editor's Note: Confectionery coating is found in the baking section of most grocery stores. It is sometimes labeled "almond bark" or "candy coating" and is often sold in bulk packages of 1 to 1-1/2 pounds.

HOLIDAY BISCOTTI
Libia Foglesong, San Bruno, California
(Pictured on page 44)

A twice-baked Italian cookie, biscotti makes a wonderful "dunker". A pretty way to present a batch is on a Christmasy plate arranged in wagon-wheel fashion.

> 1/2 cup butter *or* margarine, softened
> 1 cup sugar
> 3 eggs
> 2 teaspoons vanilla extract
> 1 teaspoon orange extract
> 3 cups all-purpose flour
> 2 teaspoons baking powder
> 1/2 teaspoon salt
> 2/3 cup dried cranberries, coarsely chopped
> 2/3 cup pistachios, coarsely chopped
> 2 tablespoons grated orange peel

In a mixing bowl, cream butter and sugar. Add eggs, one at a time, beating well after each addition. Stir in extracts. Combine flour, baking powder and salt; gradually add to creamed mixture and mix well (dough will be sticky). Stir in cranberries, pistachios and orange peel. Chill for 30 minutes. Divide dough in half. On a floured surface, shape each half into a loaf 1-1/2 to 2 in. in diameter. Place on an ungreased baking sheet. Bake at 350° for 30-35 minutes. Cool for 5 minutes. Cut diagonally into 3/4-in.-thick slices. Place slices, cut side down, on an ungreased baking sheet. Bake for 9-10 minutes. Turn slices over. Bake 10 minutes more or until golden brown. Cool on a wire rack. Store in an airtight container. **Yield:** 2 dozen.

TEXAS JALAPENO JELLY
Lori McMullen, Victoria, Texas
(Pictured above)

A jar of this jelly is always warmly appreciated...to add an extra Southwestern accent, I trim the lid with a snappy bandanna print fabric.

> 2 jalapeno peppers, seeded and chopped
> 3 medium green peppers, cut into 1-inch pieces, *divided*
> 1-1/2 cups vinegar, *divided*
> 6-1/2 cups sugar
> 1/2 to 1 teaspoon cayenne pepper
> 2 pouches (3 ounces *each*) liquid fruit pectin
> About 6 drops green food coloring, optional
> Cream cheese and crackers, optional

Puree jalapenos, half of the green peppers and 1/2 cup vinegar in a blender or food processor; pour into a large kettle. Repeat with remaining green peppers and another 1/2 cup vinegar. Add sugar, cayenne and remaining vinegar to the kettle. Bring to a rolling boil over high heat, stirring constantly. Quickly stir in pectin and return to a rolling boil. Boil for 1 minute, stirring constantly. Remove from the heat; skim off foam. Add food coloring if desired. Ladle hot liquid into hot jars, leaving 1/4-in. headspace. Cover with lids. Process for 10 minutes in a boiling-water bath. Serve over cream cheese with crackers if desired. **Yield:** 7 half-pints.

CHOCOLATE-DIPPED PRETZEL RODS
Kay Waters, Benld, Illinois
(Pictured on page 44)

Kids of all ages enjoy receiving these fun-to-eat treats for Christmas. Once the pretzels are wrapped with plastic wrap

GREAT GIFTS. Clockwise from top right: Chocolate-Dipped Pretzel Rods (p. 43), Holiday Biscotti (p. 43), Bean Soup Mix (p. 45), Peppermint Stick Sauce (p. 45) and Zesty Snack Mix (p. 45).

Peppermint Stick Sauce

ZESTY SNACK MIX
Blanche Swalwell, Thunder Bay, Ontario
(Pictured on page 44)

Friends and family hint, year after year, that they're looking forward to this well-seasoned snack mix. The sesame snack sticks and shoestring potatoes are fun surprise additions.

11 cups Cheerios
8 cups Crispix
8 cups Corn Chex
6 cups bite-size Shredded Wheat
1 package (10 ounces) corn chips
1 jar (8 ounces) salted peanuts
1 package (8 ounces) pretzel sticks
1 package (7 ounces) sesame snack sticks
1 package (7 ounces) shoestring potato sticks
1 pound butter *or* margarine
3 tablespoons garlic powder
3 tablespoons onion powder
2 tablespoons hot pepper sauce
2 tablespoons lemon juice
2 tablespoons Worcestershire sauce
2 teaspoons garlic salt

In a large bowl, combine the first nine ingredients. In a saucepan over low heat, melt butter. Add seasonings; stir until dissolved. Pour over cereal mixture; stir to coat. Place in large greased roasting pans. Bake, uncovered, at 250° for 1 hour, stirring every 15 minutes. Store in airtight containers. **Yield:** 12 quarts.

BEAN SOUP MIX
Elizabeth Clayton Paul, Nepean, Ontario
(Pictured on page 44)

An attractive bag of this savory mix makes a tasteful gift for a teacher or co-worker—remember to attach the soup recipe with a decorative ribbon or cord.

BEAN MIX:
1 cup *each* dried yellow split peas, green split peas, lentils, pearl barley, black-eyed peas, small lima beans, navy beans, great northern beans and pinto beans
SOUP:
1-1/2 quarts water
1 large onion, chopped
1 large carrot, chopped
2 teaspoons chili powder
1-1/4 teaspoons salt
1/4 teaspoon pepper
1/8 teaspoon ground cloves
1/2 pound fully cooked smoked sausage, sliced
1 can (28 ounces) diced tomatoes, undrained
1 tablespoon lemon juice

Combine bean mix ingredients. Divide into six batches, 1-1/2 cups each. Store in airtight containers. **To make one batch of soup:** Place 1-1/2 cups bean mix in a Dutch oven or soup kettle; cover with water by 2 in. Bring to a boil; boil for 2 minutes. Remove from the heat; let stand for 1 hour. Drain, discarding liquid. Return beans to kettle; add 1-1/2 qts. water. Bring to a boil. Reduce heat; cover and simmer for 1-1/2 to 2 hours or until beans are tender. Add onion, carrot, chili powder, salt, pepper and cloves. Return to a boil. Reduce heat and simmer, uncovered, for 30 minutes. Add sausage, tomatoes and lemon juice; simmer 15-20 minutes longer. **Yield:** 9 cups of mix (six batches of soup—each batch makes 2-1/2 quarts and serves 8-10).

PEPPERMINT STICK SAUCE
Linda Gronewaller, Hutchinson, Kansas
(Pictured on page 44)

This pepperminty sauce is one of my favorite Christmas gifts to give. I package it in a decorative jar, then add a container of chopped nuts to sprinkle over the topping.

1-1/2 cups finely crushed peppermint candies *or* candy canes
3/4 cup whipping cream, whipped
1 jar (7 ounces) marshmallow creme

Combine all ingredients in a medium saucepan. Cook over medium-low heat, stirring occasionally, until mixture is smooth and candy is melted. Pour into small airtight containers. Store in the refrigerator. Serve warm over ice cream or cake. **Yield:** 3 cups.

MARVELOUS MOCHA MIX
Shirley Brazel, Rocklin, California

A tin of this mix with serving instructions makes a ready-to-soothe Christmas gift. My husband and I take it to senior citizens we visit. It perks them right up!

1 cup instant chocolate drink mix
1 cup powdered nondairy creamer
2/3 cup instant coffee granules
1/2 cup sugar
1/2 teaspoon ground cinnamon
1/4 teaspoon ground nutmeg

Combine all ingredients; mix well. Store in an airtight container. **To make one serving:** Add 4-6 teaspoons mix to 3/4 cup boiling water; stir until dissolved. **Yield:** 3 cups mix (24-36 servings).

GRANDMA'S PEANUT BUTTER
Ann Teegardin, Justin, Texas

Frequently, I nestle a creamy jarful of this lip-smacking peanut butter beside homemade cookies and candy as a gift "fresh from Grandma's kitchen".

1 cup creamy peanut butter
1 cup corn syrup
1/2 cup marshmallow creme
2 tablespoons maple syrup
1 teaspoon hot water

In a mixing bowl, combine all ingredients and beat until smooth. Store in an airtight container. **Yield:** about 2 cups.

It's Time for a Christmas Barn Raising!

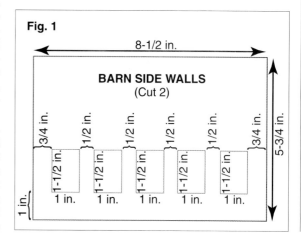

WHAT CRITTER *wouldn't* feel cozy nestled in the festive farm scene on our cover? Our *CW* test kitchen staff came up with the "plans" for this Christmas gingerbread barn...then "stocked" it with farmyard friends.

The country-as-can-be project will add a cheerful rustic touch to your holiday decor—and it's so easy to assemble you can start raising the roof right away!

GINGERBREAD BARN

DOUGH:
2-1/4 cups shortening
    2 cups sugar
    2 eggs
    1 cup molasses
    2/3 cup light corn syrup
    2 teaspoons ground ginger
1-1/2 teaspoons ground cinnamon
    1 teaspoon ground cloves
8-1/2 to 9 cups all-purpose flour
Heavy-duty cardboard
Muffin tin

In a mixing bowl, beat shortening and sugar until fluffy. Beat in eggs, molasses, corn syrup, ginger, cinnamon and cloves until well-mixed. Gradually add flour, 1 cup at a time, until the dough can be formed into a ball. Turn onto a lightly floured surface; knead until smooth and not sticky, adding more flour if needed. Cover and chill several hours or overnight.

Cut all barn patterns on page 48 out of cardboard. Cut out windows and discard. Referring to Fig. 1 at right, cut out two barn side walls (8-1/2 in. x 5-3/4 in.). If side windows are desired, cut out and discard five 1-in. x 1-1/2-in. windows measuring 1 in. from the bottom and 3/4 in. from each side, allowing 1/2 in. between windows. (Note: Roof is assembled from *cardboard*, not gingerbread.)

If farm animals are desired, cut out patterns provided on page 48 or use your favorite animal cookie cutter.

Line a baking sheet with foil and lightly grease the foil. Lay a damp towel on the counter; place prepared pan on towel (to prevent slipping). Using a lightly floured rolling pin, roll out one-sixth of the dough directly onto the baking sheet into a rectangle about 1/4 in. thick. Position a barn pattern on the dough. Using a sharp knife or pizza cutter, cut out according to quantities noted on each pattern piece; remove pattern. Remove the dough scraps; cover, refrigerate and save to reroll if needed.

Using a sharp knife, score outlines to mark the doors and windows where indicated on the pattern, being careful not to cut all the way through the dough. Score vertical lines in barn to look like siding if desired. Cut out windows where indicated.

Bake at 350° for 12-14 minutes or until edges just begin to brown. Remove from oven; immediately replace barn patterns on cookies. Cut around edges to trim off excess cookie if necessary. Cool 10 minutes or until pieces begin to firm. Carefully remove to a wire rack to cool completely. Repeat with remaining dough and patterns.

For roof of silo, cut a 5-in. circle of gingerbread. Turn a standard-size muffin tin upside down; spray the bottom of one cup with nonstick cooking spray. Mold dough circle over and down the sides of the cup, pressing together any cracks and trimming off

Fig. 1

8-1/2 in.

BARN SIDE WALLS
(Cut 2)

5-3/4 in.

3/4 in. | 1/2 in. | 1/2 in. | 1/2 in. | 1/2 in. | 3/4 in.

1-1/2 in. | 1-1/2 in. | 1-1/2 in. | 1-1/2 in. | 1-1/2 in.

1 in. | 1 in. | 1 in. | 1 in. | 1 in.

1 in.

excess dough. Bake at 350° for 10 minutes or until golden brown. Cool for 10 minutes on tin. Carefully remove to a wire rack; cool completely.

Use remaining dough for cutouts of farm animals and gingerbread people if desired. Bake cow or people cookies at 350° for 12-14 minutes and dog, chicken or pig cookies for 6-7 minutes. **Yield:** 1 barn and about 2 dozen large cookies.

ICING AND ASSEMBLY:
1-1/2 cups butter *or* margarine, softened
1-1/2 cups shortening
3/4 cup water
3 tablespoons vanilla extract
12 cups confectioners' sugar
17-inch x 22-inch display base—heavy-duty cardboard *or* cutting board *or* piece of plywood, covered with foil wrapping *or* aluminum foil
Serrated knife *or* emery board
Red, green and black liquid *or* paste food coloring
Small paintbrush
Pastry bags *or* heavy-duty resealable plastic bags
Pastry tips—#10 round, #5 round and #67 leaf
Spice bottles
Heavy-duty cardboard
Masking tape
1 package (9.5 ounces) Triscuit crackers
Cardboard roll from wrapping paper (about 10 inches long x 2-1/2 inches in diameter)
2 cups oyster crackers
Thin butter ring cookie
Decorating candies and sugars
Thin red ribbon, optional
Thin pretzel sticks
Sugar ice cream cones
Spearmint candies *or* marshmallows
Black and white jelly beans

To make icing: In a large mixing bowl, cream butter and shortening. Add water and vanilla; beat until smooth. Gradually beat in sugar; mix well. Place a damp paper towel over bowl and cover tightly between uses.

To assemble frame of the barn: Test cookie pieces to make sure they fit together snugly. If necessary, file carefully with a serrated knife or emery board to make them fit.

Combine 4 teaspoons water and 1/2 teaspoon red food coloring. Carefully brush onto front, back and sides of barn with a small paintbrush. Let

dry completely or overnight.

Insert #10 tip into pastry bag; fill two-thirds full with icing. Beginning with the back of the barn, squeeze a wide strip of icing onto the bottom edge of the back piece. Position on display base about 7 in. from one short edge. Prop it upright with spice bottles until icing is firm, about 3-4 hours.

To add barn sides and front: Squeeze icing on the lower edge of one side piece and side edge of the back piece. Align pieces at a right angle, making sure they are as tight as possible. Prop up with spice bottles. Repeat with the other side. For added stability, squeeze icing along the *inside* edge of all pieces and corners (see photo below).

Squeeze icing onto the bottom and side edges of the front piece; position with the other assembled pieces. Prop up with more spice bottles; let dry completely.

To assemble barn roof: From heavy-duty cardboard, cut two 10-1/2-in. x 3-1/2-in. pieces A. Also cut two 10-1/2-in. x 2-1/2-in. pieces B. Tape one long edge of roof pieces A and B together with masking tape; repeat. Tape both A pieces together to form center roof peak.

Squeeze icing on the upper edges of the slant of the front and back edges of the barn. Carefully place roof on the slants so that the roof's peak is even with the points of the front and back. (There will be an overhang of about 3/4 in. on the front and back.)

For roof shingles, cut Triscuits in half. Using icing, attach Triscuits to cardboard roof in rows, beginning with bottom row; slightly overlap each row, alternating shingle seams (see photo at right). Repeat for other side. Cut narrow strips of crackers and attach to center of roof peak.

To make silo: Coat cardboard roll with icing; press one side of oyster

crackers into icing to cover entire silo. Squeeze icing onto the top edge of the silo; carefully press gingerbread silo roof onto the silo. Squeeze icing onto lower edge of silo; stand it upright at the corner of the barn.

To decorate barn: Using a #5 tip, outline windows and doors with white icing. Tint a portion of the icing with green food coloring; use the leaf tip to decorate a butter ring cookie to make a wreath. Add decorating candies or ribbon if desired. Attach wreath to barn with icing.

Combine 1/2 teaspoon water with a small amount of green food coloring; brush onto shutters. Attach to sides of small window on barn front with icing. Pipe icicles on barn and silo roofs with icing. If desired, frost base around barn and silo to create snow.

To make barnyard fence: Overlap ends of pretzel sticks at desired angles; fasten together at intersections with dabs of icing. Let dry until icing is firm, about 1 hour. (If you're having difficulty making the icing hold— *and you're planning on using your barn for show only*—use white glue to adhere pretzels together.)

Arrange fence around barn and attach with icing.

Add finishing touches: To make trees, use a serrated knife to carefully score and cut sugar ice cream cones to desired heights.

Tint a portion of icing with green food coloring; decorate trees using the leaf tip. Use spearmint candies for shrubs or decorate marshmallows with leaf tip. When frosting is dry, arrange as desired and attach to base with icing.

To frost markings on barnyard animals, thin a small portion of the icing with water; add black food coloring. Paint markings on animals as desired. Allow to dry. Position animals around the barn; secure with dabs of icing.

To make path, cut jelly beans in half lengthwise; arrange with cut side down and adhere to board with icing.
(Barn patterns are on next page)

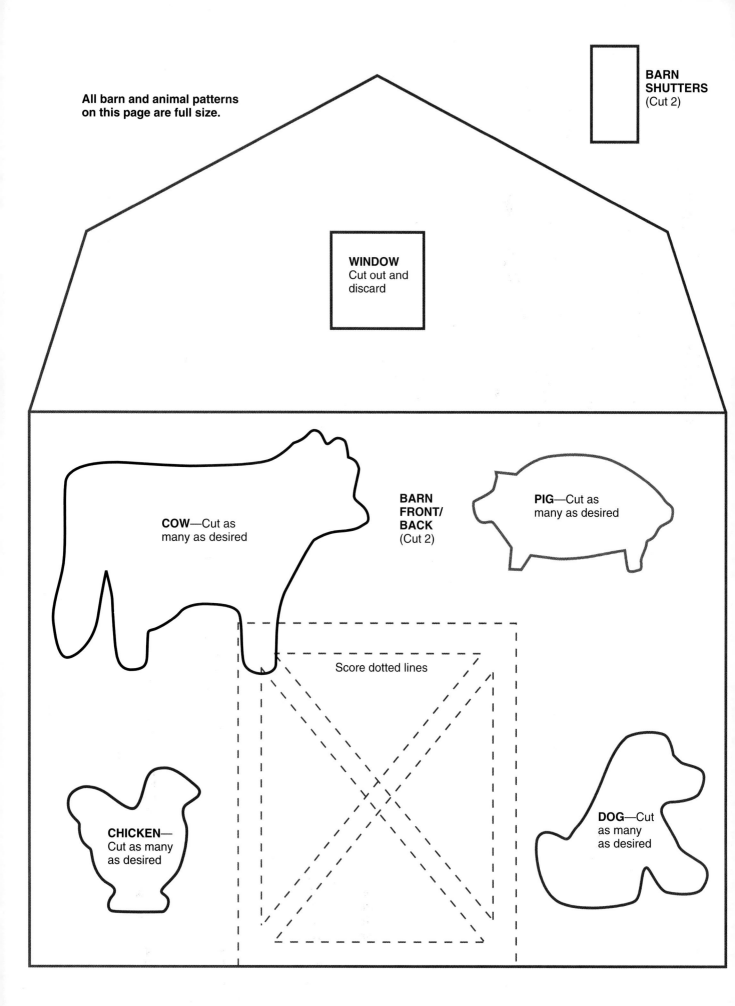

BARN SHUTTERS (Cut 2)

All barn and animal patterns on this page are full size.

WINDOW Cut out and discard

COW—Cut as many as desired

BARN FRONT/BACK (Cut 2)

PIG—Cut as many as desired

Score dotted lines

CHICKEN— Cut as many as desired

DOG—Cut as many as desired

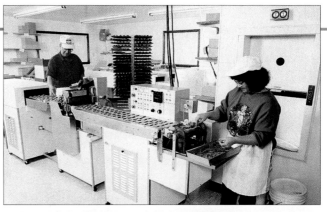

Sweetenin' the Season Is at Center of Family Tradition

COUNT Myrna Wolf among the country women who are most sweet on Christmas. Her family's holidays are filled with sugar and spice…and *lots* of chocolate.

Myrna and husband Jim have kept the delicious confections coming for decade after decade at Wolf's Homemade Candies in Attica, Indiana. In all, they cook up about 30,000 pounds of chocolate a year.

"We make over 60 varieties of toffees, chocolate cream candies, fudge, caramels and chocolate-covered nuts," Myrna tallies. "Our two best-sellers are our chocolate-covered toffee and our chocolate-covered caramel and pecan specialties. People elsewhere call them turtles…but around here, they're known as 'Wolfies'!"

Myrna and Jim readily admit they love to sample the sweet fruits of their labor. In fact, chocolate has become such a family affair that one of their two grown daughters, Candace, runs a second Wolf's store in Lenexa, Kansas.

"I was a year old when my parents became candy makers," she reminisces. "How could I *not* love chocolate?"

Adding old-fashioned dash to their candies, Myrna and Jim's stove dates back 80 years. They still cook their confections in copper kettles, and they stir the candy with maple paddles. What's more, they use only natural ingredients —chocolate, sugar, nuts, fruits, butter and oils—and no preservatives.

They are glad, however, to turn to one modern convenience.

"Making candy is a tricky procedure," Myrna notes. "The conditions have to be just right. High humidity, for instance, can ruin an entire batch. So we're the only folks in town who run the air conditioner in winter!"

Since their candy can't stand the heat, the Wolfs close shop for 6 weeks during the hot Hoosier summer. The annual hiatus also helps them rest up for the holiday rush. During autumn, when they are preparing for their seasonal scurry, their busy days regularly stretch to 12 to 16 hours.

There's a sweet reward for all that

MMM-ERRY CHRISTMAS. Myrna Wolf (top left) and husband Jim (above) are sweet on the season. Over the holidays, they turn out chocolaty specialties the old-fashioned way.

hard work, though. "In the 30 years we've been making candy," Myrna reports, "we have never had a single complaint or return."

How's that for confection perfection?

Editor's Note: *Wolf's Homemade Candies is located at 503 S. Council, U.S. 41, Attica IN 47918. To order by telephone, call 1-317/762-6707.* ❀

49

Christmas Present Of Past Wraps up Her Whole House

COME CHRISTMAS at Iris Riley's, it's out with the *new* and in with the *old*.

Iris spends the year collecting treasures from Christmases past—antique sleds, spindle and gourd Santas and more vintage items dating back as far as the 1880's. Then she tucks them in every corner of the two-bedroom house in Norwalk, Ohio she and her husband, Tim, have made their home.

"You know the excitement of a child eager for Christmas to come?" Iris smiles. "It's exactly how I feel before the holidays. I can't wait to bring out my favorite decorations."

That's obvious from the first step you set in her house—a crew of skinny fence-post Santas greets visitors in the front entryway. As you walk from room to room, though, you soon see Iris doesn't believe good things come only in small packages. "I have nine antique trunks," she details, "and I open them all to use for decorating."

One trunk in the master bedroom is full of the Dickens—Charles, himself, that is! Stuffed dolls of Tiny Tim and other characters the English author created for his classic *A Christmas Carol* tale enjoy a holiday dinner in what was once a doll case. At the foot of the four-poster bed, rosy-cheeked carolers make merry in a larger trunk.

Santas, however, are definitely the stars here. Hundreds made from stairway spindles, table legs and—like those in the front entryway—fence posts populate the place with their Christmas spirit. Some as tiny as a candle taper sit atop the fireplace mantel. Another, set near the staircase, stretches to an astounding height of 9 feet.

The Yuletide flourishes fit right in all over, too. When the Rileys' house was built a decade ago, Iris looked ahead to her favorite season and made sure to select colors easily dressed for the holidays: emerald green and taupe in the master bedroom and den, soft peach and country blue in the dining room.

Speaking of that sunny room, the ornate sideboard that stands against a

wall is a favorite conversation piece, Iris says. She decorates it for December with poinsettias...but she knows all eyes in the dining room are on the presents stowed underneath!

Well-weathered sleighs round out Iris' Christmas riches. One does double duty as a television stand, while a companion has been transformed into a coffee table.

That Amish-crafted sleigh was originally used to haul firewood. Even now, it carries warming cargo—a decorative Santa riding a small-scale sleigh.

Look close and you'll notice the jolly old man is smiling under his bushy white beard. And why not? He feels right at home here in Iris' appealingly oldfangled country abode! ❧

MAKING MERRY for Iris Riley (above) means setting holiday scene with evergreens, gourdgeous St. Nicks, paper-twist carolers and more. Outdoors, gazebo's Christmas spirit is "flagging".

CHRISTMAS TRADITION at the Rileys' calls for sprucing up every room. Moving clockwise from top left, tree-mendous centerpiece starts festive feeling branching out around the house while spindle Santas stand sentry at hearthside. Old-time trunks can't keep a lid on Yuletide stories, restored sleds pull their weight as display tables—even bedrooms are blanketed with holiday style.

A Quilt for Jesus

A fiction story by Carol Ritten Smith of Innisfail, Alberta

FINALLY it was December 24—Christmas Eve and the grandchildren had all arrived. Helen *was* happy. Still, a nagging concern threatened her family's enjoyment of this most special of the holidays:

Santa's impending visit, of course, had the youngsters excited. What troubled Helen, though, was that not one of them had breathed a single word about the real meaning of Christmas, what had happened long ago in a humble stable.

Stable? That gave Helen an idea—the barn!

"Molly" mooed gently as Helen and her grandchildren entered the cows' home. Helen sat down on a bale of hay. Beth, 2, and Kendall, 5, crawled onto her lap. Tracy, 8, and Tyler, 10, snuggled close on either side.

"If we hung up a stocking for Molly, do you think Santa would fill it?" asked Tracy.

"Maybe," Helen chuckled. "But, because this is kind of like a stable, I have a question for all of you—can you tell me the story of the first Christmas?"

"Don't you know it yet, Grandma?" questioned Tracy, her brown eyes widening in amazement.

" 'Course she knows it," Tyler piped up impatiently. "Everyone knows it."

"Well, then," Helen suggested, "since you're the oldest, Tyler, why don't you go first?"

Straightening his shoulders, the boy began, "Once upon a time…"

"It's not a fairy tale," Tracy interrupted. "You're supposed to say, 'And it came to pass'."

"I can start it any way I want," her brother insisted. "Once upon a time, there was this lady named Mary and she…"

Despite the dubious beginning, the basics of the Christmas story were all there: Mary and Joseph and, of course, the Baby…the manger, the star of Bethlehem…shepherds, wise men and King Herod. Tracy and Kendall inserted a few words, while Beth listened intently, sucking her thumb.

Pleased with what she'd heard, Helen pressed on. "If each of you were to give a gift to the Baby Jesus," she wondered, "what would it be?"

"A nose plug," responded Tyler immediately. "Barns stink. That's why the wise men brought Him fancy perfumes."

"I know," offered Tracy. "I'd give baby clothes. All Mary had to wrap Him in was swathing clothes."

"Swaddling clothes," Tyler corrected.

"I gib da baby my dolly," Kendall reported proudly.

"Humph," grumbled Tyler. "I'd give Him something better than a dumb doll!"

"And what would that be—besides a nose plug?" Helen smiled in encouragement.

After some deliberation, he replied, "I'd give Him my toy hammer and saw. Jesus grew up to be a carpenter. So I'd give Him His first set of tools."

Helen nodded in satisfaction. "I'm sure Jesus would be very happy with all your gifts."

"Grandma?" Tracy inquired. "What would you give Him?"

Whoa! Helen hadn't expected to have her question volleyed back. What would she give Him? It would have to be very special, something with great meaning to show how much she loved Him…

"I know, I know!" announced Tracy, her hand raised as if she were about to answer a question in school. "You could make Him a quilt like you made for each of us, with His name and birth date stitched on it."

Oh, yes, a baby quilt would be perfect, unique and made with love, Helen thought. What could be a better gift than that? "You're right, Tracy," she agreed.

"Yeah, then He could have His own blankie," Tyler concurred with a solemn nod.

"Bankie," Beth sighed sleepily, rubbing her eyes. "Me want bankie."

"I think she's just about ready for her nap," Tracy observed in a motherly fashion.

"I think so, too," Helen said. "We had better start back to the house now."

And, all the way there, Helen silently pondered just one thing—which blocks to choose for the most important quilt that she would ever make. ✿

Readers' Poetry Corner

Christmas Collage

Christmas is candles and new-fallen snow,
Christmas is holly and fresh mistletoe;
It's trimming the tree and decking the hall
And shopping for gifts at the nearest mall.

It's carolers strolling down the street,
And wishing "Merry Christmas" to folks
  you meet;
Christmas is a tree with a star perched high,
Lights winking and blinking at passersby.

It's going to church on Christmas Eve
To watch young children play make-believe
With gauzy wings and halos on heads;
It's an infant child asleep in His bed.

Christmas is secrets and whispers and such,
Gaily wrapped packages you mustn't
  touch;
All this and much more is surely the reason
Christmas isn't just a day...it's a season!

—Berniece Phillips
Cuba, Illinois

Christmas Greetings Are Covered with Quick Cards

HERE'S a noteworthy idea—crafter Paula Del Favero of Deerfield Beach, Florida shares a pair of pleasing greeting cards you can put together to spread Christmas cheer this year.

Materials Needed (for both cards):
Patterns on next page
5-inch x 7-inch blank cards (sold in stationery and art supply stores and card shops) or 14-inch x 10-inch piece of heavy paper (medium-weight watercolor paper, card stock or construction paper)
Matching envelopes
Scraps of cotton Christmas fabrics— one 6-inch x 8-inch piece of red and green print for each gift box card; one 6-inch x 8-inch piece of blue snowman print and scrap of red print for each snowman card
14 inches of 3/4-inch-wide red ribbon
One 3/4-inch white button
1/4-inch pom-poms—five black and one green
Fine-line permanent markers—black and red

1/4 yard of paper-backed fusible web
Pencil
Scissors
Tape measure
Tacky (white) glue
Iron and ironing surface
Press cloth
Kitchen parchment paper or Teflon applique press sheet
Ruler

Finished Size: Each card is 5 inches x 7 inches.

Directions:
If not using blank cards, fold heavy white paper in half lengthwise so it measures 14 in. x 5 in. Make a sharp crease along fold. Cut folded paper in half to make two 7-in. x 5-in. cards. Set aside.

Cut a 6-in. x 8-in. fabric scrap along the grain line for each card. Set aside.

Cut two 5-3/4-in. x 7-3/4-in. pieces of paper-backed fusible web. Set aside.

GIFT BOX CARD: Preheat iron to medium (permanent press, no steam) setting. Place gift box card fabric wrong side up on ironing surface. Center paper-backed fusible web on top of fabric. Cover with press cloth. Press fusible web onto fabric, following manufacturer's directions. Allow to cool.

Remove paper backing. Trim extra fabric from one long edge, cutting straight along grain line. Position this cut edge along folded edge of card with right side of fabric up and fusible web next to card. Protect ironing surface with kitchen parchment paper or applique sheet and fuse fabric to card. Allow to cool.

Cut red ribbon into one 8-in. piece and one 6-in. piece.

Position ribbon pieces on top of card as shown in photo at left, allowing the ends to extend beyond each edge. Glue in place.

Open card and trim away excess fabric, carefully cutting along outside edge of card with scissors. Fold card along crease and re-trim edges if necessary. (Do not cut along fold!)

Glue button on front of card at intersection of ribbons as shown in photo.

SNOWMAN CARD: Repeat Gift Box Card directions for fusing paper-backed fusible web to wrong side of snowman fabric. Trim extra fabric from one long edge, cutting straight along grain line.

Trace snowman body pattern and center mark onto tracing paper. Cut out. Place pattern on paper side of fused snowman fabric, positioning center mark 2-1/2 in. from trimmed edge and 4 in. from top edge. Trace around pattern. Carefully snip through fused fabric at center of traced pattern, then cut shape out from center of fabric to create a silhouette. Discard cutout piece.

Remove paper backing from fabric and fuse to card, following Gift Box Card directions above.

Open card and trim away excess fabric, carefully cutting along outside edge of card with scissors. Fold card along crease and re-trim edges if necessary. (Do not cut along fold!)

Trace hat, nose and bow tie patterns onto paper side of fusible web and fuse onto wrong side of red print fabric. Cut out hat, nose and bow tie.

Remove paper backing and position hat, nose and bow tie on snowman as shown on photo. Fuse into place.

Use black marker to draw dots for mouth as shown on pattern and stitching lines around snowman as shown in photo.

Use red marker to draw heart on snowman as indicated on pattern.

Glue black pom-pom eyes and buttons on snowman and green pom-pom tip on hat as indicated on pattern. ❄

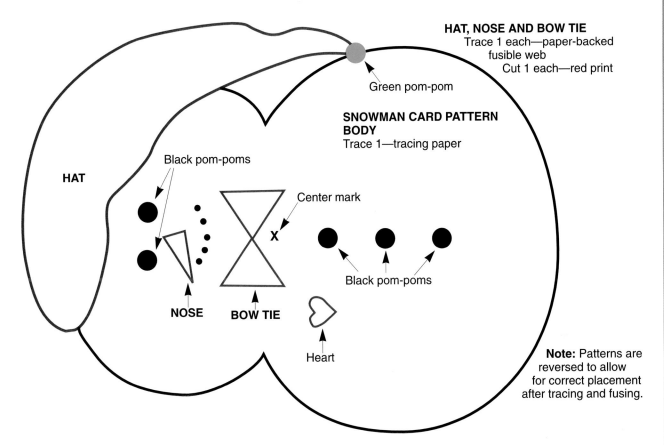

HAT, NOSE AND BOW TIE
Trace 1 each—paper-backed
fusible web
Cut 1 each—red print

Green pom-pom

SNOWMAN CARD PATTERN
BODY
Trace 1—tracing paper

Black pom-poms

HAT

Center mark

X

Black pom-poms

NOSE   **BOW TIE**

Heart

Note: Patterns are
reversed to allow
for correct placement
after tracing and fusing.

Earmark Your Fabric Scraps for Yuletide Fashion

ACCESSORIES for your Christmas outfit are a nice idea...but they can be expensive. That makes these easy-on-the-budget (and the eyes) earrings from Bette Veinot of Bridgewater, Nova Scotia especially appealing. To make them, you use fabric scraps.

Materials Needed (for one pair of earrings):
Two 2-1/2-inch circles of Christmas print or plaid fabric
Two 1-inch circles of felt in color to match fabric
Two 1-1/4-inch circles of velour or fleece
Two 1-1/4-inch circles cut from plastic lid
Two 10mm flat-pad earring posts with clutches or two flat-pad clip earring backs
Waterproof (washable) craft glue
Matching thread
Standard sewing supplies

Finished Size: Each earring is about 1-1/4 inches across.

Directions:
Glue one velour or fleece circle to each plastic circle. Let dry.

Trim velour or fleece close to plastic if necessary.

With matching thread, sew small running stitches 1/8 in. from outside edge of each fabric earring circle, leaving long threads for gathering. See Fig. 1 for running stitch. (Do not turn edge of fabric under.)

Center one velour or fleece side of plastic circle on the wrong side of each fabric circle. Pull long threads ends to gather fabric tightly around plastic circles. Knot to secure threads and trim ends close. Smooth gathers along outside edges of earrings.

Center felt circle on back of each fabric circle and glue. Let dry.

Glue an earring back to the top edge of each felt circle. ❄

Fig. 1

Running stitch

Craft Cute Paper Twist Choir Kids...for a Song!

THESE colorful choristers, humming their hearts out, are sure to bring joy to the world—in song and sight! They're easy enough to twist up in an afternoon, too, shares handcrafter Kathy Rankin of Waukesha, Wisconsin.

Whether "performing" from a tabletop or staircase, the characters can be counted on to strike a chord with your country decor. Either way, they will start the holidays on the right note!

Materials needed (for each kid):
Pattern on next page
Tracing paper
Pencil
4-inch-wide paper twist—3-1/2 yards of white and 1-1/2 yards of off-white
Styrofoam—one 3-1/2-inch ball and one 12-inch x 4-inch cone
Wooden doll pin or round clothespin
Two 9-inch pieces of white pipe cleaner
13-inch piece of 16-gauge wire
Small amount of polyester stuffing
Fine-line permanent black marker
Ruler
Craft scissors
Wire cutter
Glue gun and glue sticks
Tacky (white) glue
Waxed paper
Rubber band
24-gauge craft wire
Powdered blush
Cotton swab
6-3/8-inch x 3-1/2-inch piece of lightweight white cardboard

Materials needed (for choir girl):
4-inch-wide paper twist—4-1/2 yards of red and 7-1/2 inches of green
Two packages (.9 ounce each) of curly doll hair in color of choice
1-1/2 yards of white 5/8-inch- or 3/4-inch-wide flat lace

Materials needed (for choir boy):
4-inch-wide paper twist—4-1/4 yards of green and 7-1/2 inches of red
One package (.9 ounce) of curly doll hair in color of choice.

Finished Size: Each choir kid is about 16 inches tall.

Directions:

PAPER TWIST: If there is a right side to the paper twist pieces, it is generally the darker and shinier side. If you prefer the other side, just make sure to use the same side throughout the project.

Cut end refers to the crosswise end. Side and edge refer to the finished edge as it comes from the factory or the trimmed lengthwise edge of the paper.

After cutting, untwist all of the cut paper twist pieces, flattening them as much as possible.

Paper-twist gluing is done with tacky glue. Glue pieces together, overlapping side edges by 1/4 to 1/2 in. Put a piece of waxed paper inside tubes when gluing final seams to prevent layers from sticking together.

HEADS (Both): Push lower end of doll pin or clothespin into top of cone as in Fig. 1. Glue into cone.

Push top end of doll pin or clothespin halfway into Styrofoam ball for head, leaving a 1/2-in. gap between ball and cone. Glue in place.

Cut one 12-in. and one 15-in. piece of off-white paper twist. Untwist both pieces. Glue the 12-in. piece centered lengthwise over top of ball, covering as much of the ball as possible.

Make a twist in center of 15-in. off-white paper twist piece. Glue the twisted area to top of ball so ends extend across 12-in. piece. Bring ends down, flattening piece out to cover remainder of ball and ends and edges of 12-in. piece. Glue edges in place and gather ends together around pin. Glue to pin and cone at base of head to form neck. Twist the rubber band around paper twist at neck to secure.

GOWN: Girl: Cut two 9-1/2-in. pieces and six 11-in. pieces of red paper twist. Untwist all pieces.

To cover cone bottom, glue the two 9-1/2-in. pieces together side by side. Let dry. Place the cone in the center of the glued pieces and glue to the bottom and up the sides of the cone.

Glue edges of five of the 11-in. pieces together side by side, forming about an 18-in. x 11-in. piece.

For the hem, fold 1-1/2 in. of one long edge to the wrong side. Glue in place. Let dry.

With hemmed edge of gown piece touching tabletop, gather up top edge of gown piece to fit cone. Glue top edge in place with edges overlapping 1/2 in. at center back.

Wrap remaining 11-in. piece around to cover top of cone and upper edge of gown piece. Trim to fit and glue in place.

Boy: Repeat as directed above, using green paper twist.

HANDS (Both): Trace hand pattern onto tracing paper and cut out. Cut two 4-1/2-in.-long pieces of off-white paper twist. Untwist both. Trace hand pattern onto wrong sides of both paper twist pieces. Cut out.

Mark pipe cleaner placement line on wrong side of one hand shape as shown on hand pattern. Curve one pipe cleaner to follow pipe cleaner placement line. Run a bead of tacky glue along pipe cleaner placement line on hand shape. Place pipe cleaner on top of glue line, making sure that pipe cleaner adheres to paper twist along placement line.

Add another bead of glue to top and outside edges of pipe cleaner. Press hand with pipe cleaner to wrong side of other hand shape, matching edges. Press outside edges together until glue sets. Let dry. Trim hand shape and ends of pipe cleaner as needed.

Repeat for remaining hands of girl and boy.

Gather and glue open ends of hands together. Push an end of 16-gauge wire piece between the layers of each hand before glue sets, gluing 1 in. of wire inside. Wrap 24-gauge wire around each hand 1/2 in. from cut edge (Fig. 2).

GOWN SLEEVES: Girl: Cut four 8-

in. pieces of red paper twist. Untwist. Glue side edges of two pieces together, wrong sides out, forming one tube for each gown sleeve. Let dry. Slide a gown sleeve tube over hand and wind 24-gauge wire around base of hand and sleeve as shown in Fig. 2. Pull tube back over hand, bringing end to center of wire. Lightly stuff 3 in. of gown sleeve. Repeat for second sleeve and wire sleeves together at center.

Boy: Repeat girl gown sleeves, except use green paper twist.

TOP SLEEVES: Girl: Cut three 16-in. pieces of white paper twist. Untwist. Glue side edges together, right side out, forming a tube. Let dry.

For hems, fold and glue 1-1/2 in. of both ends to inside of tube. Glue lace to inside lower edge of each sleeve, allowing 1/2 in. of lace to extend out and overlapping ends 1/2 in.

Slide hands/gown sleeves inside top sleeves, allowing hands to extend out evenly on each end. Gather together at the center and glue center to top back of cone, making sure both hands have thumbs pointing up.

Boy: Repeat girl top sleeves, forming 1-in. hems instead and omitting lace.

TOP: Girl: Cut six 9-in. pieces of white paper twist. Untwist. Glue edges of three of the pieces together side by side, forming about an 11-in. x 9-in. piece. Gather one 11-in. end of this set of pieces together and glue to front at neck, covering front of gown from sleeve to sleeve. Repeat for back.

Glue front edges over back edges under arms.

Fold 1-1/2 in. to inside and glue in place for hem. Glue lace to inside edge of hem, allowing 1/2 in. of lace to extend out and overlapping ends 1/2 in. in back.

Boy: Repeat girl top, forming 1-in. hem and omitting lace.

COLLAR: Girl: Cut four 3-1/2-in. pieces of white paper twist. Untwist. Glue pieces together side by side, forming a 14-in. x 3-1/2-in. piece. Fold under 1 in. along one long edge and glue in place for hem.

Glue lace to inside edge of hem, allowing 1/2 in. of lace to extend out. Gather other edge of collar and glue to neck, placing opening at center front.

Boy: Repeat girl collar, forming 1-1/2-in. hem instead and omitting lace.

BOW: Girl: Cut a 22-in. piece of red paper twist. Untwist. Cut piece in half lengthwise and fold one half-width piece as shown in Fig. 3, forming a 4-1/2-in.-wide bow. Cut a 1-1/2-in. piece from remaining half-width piece to form bow center. Wrap short piece around center of bow and glue ends to back of bow.

Glue bow to girl's neck with ends hanging down. Cut ends in an inverted V shape.

Boy: Cut a 10-in. piece of green paper twist. Untwist. Cut piece in half lengthwise and using one half-width piece, fold ends to overlap 1/2 in. at center. Cut a 2-1/2-in. piece from remaining half-width piece to form the bow center. Wrap the short piece around center of the bow, covering ends, and glue ends of bow center to back of bow. Glue the bow to boy's neck.

HAIR: Girl: Pull out three to four strands of curls and cut into 9-in. lengths. Fold at midpoint of cut lengths, leaving cut ends hanging down.

Use glue gun to apply a dab of glue to back of girl's head about 2 in. above neckline and press fold of curls into glue. Hold in place until glue sets.

Repeat around sides to edge of face, then add another row of curls 1 in. above first row of curls. Repeat until head is covered with curls, using shorter strands to cover top. Untangle curls and trim to desired length.

Boy: Cut 1-in. pieces of curly hair. Add a dot of glue to boy's head 1 in. above back of neck and push end of one piece of curly hair into glue. Repeat to add curls across head to edge of face. Add additional rows to cover remainder of head with curls.

FACE (Both): Use black marker to add eyelashes, nose and mouth to each face as shown in photo. Use cotton swab to add blush to cheeks.

CHOIR BOOKS: Girl: For cover, cut a 7-1/2-in. piece of green paper twist. Untwist. Center cardboard piece on wrong side of green paper twist piece. Fold corners of paper twist over corners of cardboard piece and glue in place, then fold and glue all edges in.

Cut a 7-1/4-in. piece of white paper twist. Untwist. Fold edges to wrong side to form a 6-1/4-in. x 3-3/8-in. rectangle. Center, right side up, on inside of book, covering inside edges of cover and glue into place.

Fold book in half crosswise, cover side out. Use black marker to write "JOY TO THE WORLD" on front cover.

Bend arms to hold choir book between hands and glue in place.

Boy: Repeat as for girl choir book, using red paper twist. ❀

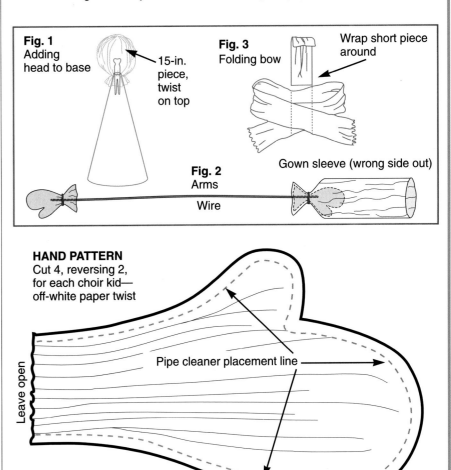

Fig. 1 Adding head to base — 15-in. piece, twist on top

Fig. 2 Arms — Wire

Fig. 3 Folding bow — Wrap short piece around

Gown sleeve (wrong side out)

HAND PATTERN
Cut 4, reversing 2, for each choir kid—off-white paper twist

Leave open

Pipe cleaner placement line

Simple Trim Brightens up Decor

HERE'S an idea to illuminate your holidays—no matter how you use it.

Of course, you can string the garland along the mantel or around the tree. But Julie Todd of Aurelia, Iowa also advises that her stars look pretty dangling around a door jamb.

Materials Needed:

Pattern on this page
Tracing or pattern paper
Pencil
Cotton fabric scraps—two 4-inch squares for each of nine stars (18 squares total) in assorted red and green Christmas prints
12-inch square of batting
Vanishing or erasable fabric markers— one light and one dark
Red and green thread
1/4-inch pony or barrel beads—eight red and eight green
Eight 3/8-inch jingle bells
60 inches of 1/8-inch-wide red satin ribbon
Pinking shears
Size 16 tapestry needle
Standard sewing supplies

Finished Size: Garland is 36 inches long.

Directions:
FABRIC STARS: Cut nine 4-in. squares of batting.

Trace star pattern onto tracing or pattern paper and cut out pattern.

Using dark vanishing or erasable marker for light prints and light marker for dark prints, trace around star pattern on right side of one 4-in. fabric square.

Place matching fabric square wrong side up on a flat surface. Place a batting square on top of fabric. Place fabric square with star tracing right side up on top of batting. Match all edges. Pin through layers as needed to hold squares together for sewing.

Starting at a point on the star, machine-stitch over traced lines with contrasting thread. Backstitch at the beginning and end to secure threads. Pivot star with needle in the down position to make accurate points. Trim threads.

Trim 1/4 in. outside stitching lines with pinking shears.

Repeat for remaining eight stars.

GARLAND: Tie a knot 12 in. from one end of red ribbon and thread needle with opposite end of ribbon.

Insert threaded needle at one star point between the top and bottom fabric layers, making sure not to pierce the bottom fabric layer. Push the needle through the batting and bring it out at the opposite point (see Fig. 1). The ribbon should not show through the main part of the star. Slide the star down the ribbon to the knotted end.

Thread on a green bead, a jingle

bell and a red bead, and slide each down the ribbon to the star.

Repeat with remaining stars, beads and bells. After adding the final star, tie a knot next to the point of the last star. There should be about a 12-in. ribbon tail left. Use ribbon tails at both ends for tying the garland to a doorway, tree, another garland, etc. ✿

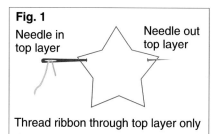

Fig. 1
Needle in top layer
Needle out top layer
Thread ribbon through top layer only

FABRIC STAR PATTERN
Trace 9—assorted red and green Christmas prints

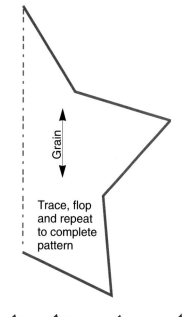

Grain

Trace, flop and repeat to complete pattern

Sprightly Snowmen Animate Boughs of Tree

THIS CHRISTMAS, you can make a trio of jolly, happy souls as freshly festive as Frosty himself—and stay toasty and warm indoors!

It's a cinch with these clever cross-stitch designs from Michele Crawford of Spokane, Washington. Trim your tree with the colorful crew, then relax— Michele's snowmen are guaranteed to keep their shape all season long.

Materials Needed (for all three ornaments):
Charts on next page
9-inch x 12-inch sheet of white 14-count Aida Plus fabric*
J&P Coats or Anchor six-strand embroidery floss in colors listed on color key
Size 24 tapestry needle
1-inch gold star button
Water-soluble pen

Scissors
Ruler
*Michele used Zweigart Aida Plus fabric, which is available in most craft stores. If you can't find the fabric in your area, you can order it from The American Needlewoman, P.O. Box 6472, Ft. Worth TX 76115, 1-800/433-2231.

Finished Size: Each ornament measures about 2-1/4 inches wide x 3-3/8

inches high. Design area is 30 stitches wide x 45 stitches high.

Special Notes: Aida Plus fabric has a specially bonded backing, which keeps the fabric from fraying when you cut it. There is no need to zigzag or overcast the edges of the fabric before you start stitching unless you choose to use a fabric other than Aida Plus.

Directions:
Cut a 3-in. x 4-in. piece of Aida Plus for each ornament. Measure and mark center of each piece of Aida Plus with water-soluble pen. To find center of chart, draw lines across the chart, connecting the arrows. Begin stitching at this point so design will be centered.

Separate floss and use two strands for cross-stitching and one strand for backstitching as shown in Fig. 1.

Each square on the chart equals one stitch over a set of fabric threads, with different colors and/or symbols representing different colors or stitches. Use the colors indicated on the color key and follow the chart to first complete the cross-stitching, then the backstitching.

Do not knot floss. Instead, leave a short tail on back of work and hold in place. Weave tails and ends through several stitches as stitching progresses.

FINISHING: Cut one square beyond stitched design around snowman.

Fold a 4-1/2-in. length of Bright Red floss in half. Sew center of folded piece to top center back of ornament. Tie ends in overhand knot to form hanger. Repeat with other two ornaments.

Snowman 1: Tie a small bow using six-strand Bright Green floss and sew it to the top of the package.

Snowman 2: Sew the gold star button between the snowman's mittens, referring to photo for placement. ❋

Fig. 1

Cross-stitch   Backstitch

SNOWMEN ORNAMENTS

COLOR KEY	J&P Coats	Anchor
☐ Canary Deep	2298	298
☒ Burnt Orange	2330	330
■ Bright Red	3046	46
⊙ Light Cranberry	3151	50
▨ Bright Green	6227	227
■ Black	8403	403
BACKSTITCHING		
— Bright Red	3046	46
— Bright Green	6227	227
— Black	8403	403

SNOWMAN 1

SNOWMAN 2

SNOWMAN 3

Craft Section...

Young Ones Will Glow Over 'Endeering' Outfits

CHILDREN are sure to take a shine to these garments—you stitch Santa's favorite reindeer right onto them.

Avon Mackay of Waukesha, Wisconsin, who herded together this critter craft, reveals that her designs work well on already-made clothing or commercial patterns you sew yourself. Meanwhile, leftover fabrics will fill out the appliques beautifully.

Materials Needed (for both outfits):
Patterns on next page
Tracing or pattern paper
Pencil
Garments—red sweatshirt for boy and red dropped-waist sweatshirt dress for girl (either make these yourself from commercial patterns or purchase them)
100% cotton fabrics—1/4 yard or scraps of dark tan for reindeer heads; scrap of red plaid for boy's reindeer bow tie; 2/3 yard of red plaid for girl's reindeer bow; scraps of dark brown, red and green
All-purpose sewing thread—red, brown, green, white and color to complement red plaid
1/2 yard of paper-backed fusible web
1/2 yard of tear-away stabilizer or typing paper
Black embroidery thread
No. 24 chenille needle
Standard sewing supplies

Finished Size: The reindeer applique measures about 7 inches wide x 10 inches tall and will fit on most garments for both children and adults. It can also be reduced on a copy machine to fit on baby-size apparel.

Directions:
Pre-wash fabrics, washing all colors separately. If water from fabrics is discolored, wash again until rinse water runs clear. Machine-dry and press all fabrics.

Wash and dry sweatshirt garments following manufacturer's instructions. If desired, remove ribbing from bottom of boy's sweatshirt and machine-stitch a 1-1/4-in. hem to wrong side of garment.

Open side seams on purchased garments for ease in appliqueing. If you choose to sew your own sweatshirt garments, applique the motif to garment front before stitching side seams.

APPLIQUEING: Trace patterns onto tracing or pattern paper, adding under-laps as indicated by dotted lines on patterns. Cut out all patterns.

Cut pieces of paper-backed fusible web a bit larger than each pattern piece. Following manufacturer's instructions, fuse paper-backed fusible web onto wrong side of fabrics as indicated.

Place pattern pieces onto paper side of fused fabrics. Trace around pattern pieces as indicated on patterns. For each reindeer, cut one head, two antlers and one nose. For the girl's reindeer only, cut holly. For the boy's reindeer only, cut one bow tie.

Transfer stitching lines for mouth, eyes and eyebrows by machine-stitching through lines traced on paper backing. Remove paper backing.

Center top of each reindeer's head about 4-1/2 in. below neckline ribbing seam on front of each garment. Tuck antlers under each reindeer head to under-lap line. Center bow tie for boy's reindeer over bottom edge of neck and place holly at bottom of left antler for girl's reindeer. Fuse all pieces into place on each garment according to manufacturer's instructions.

Position tear-away stabilizer or typing paper on back side of garment fabric behind applique areas. Using appropriate thread color and a medium satin zigzag setting on your sewing machine, applique pieces to front of garment in this order: antlers, neck, head, face, holly for girl's reindeer and bow tie for boy's reindeer.

Using red thread and medium satin zigzag setting, applique red nose on each reindeer and stitch three holly berries on girl's reindeer. Remove tear-away stabilizer from back of garments. Pull all threads to back and secure.

EMBROIDERY: Sep-arate six-strand black embroidery floss and use three strands for all embroidery. Following stitching lines, use backstitch (Fig. 1) to hand-embroider holly veins, eyebrows and mouth. Hand-embroider eyes using satin stitch (Fig. 2).

FABRIC BOW (for girl's reindeer): Cut a 28-in. x 5-1/2-in. piece on bias from plaid. Fold in half lengthwise with right sides together and cut ends at 45° angle. Pin raw edges and stitch a 1/4-in. seam, leaving a 2-in. opening at the center for turning.

Trim bow points close to stitching in order to reduce bulk. Turn right side out. Gently work fabric to make a sharp point at the bow ends. Press bow. Hand-stitch opening closed. Fold into 7-in. bow as shown in photo and pin on the reindeer's neck as indicated on the pattern.

Bow knot: Cut a 1-1/2-in. x 2-1/2-in. bias piece from plaid fabric. Fold in half lengthwise with right sides together and stitch a 1/4-in. seam along long edge.

Turn right side out and center seam. Wrap bow knot over center of bow with seam to back and hand-stitch raw edges together on back of bow.

Center bow on right side of garment at bottom of reindeer neck. Pin in place and machine- or hand-stitch on garment, hiding stitches under bow knot. ❈

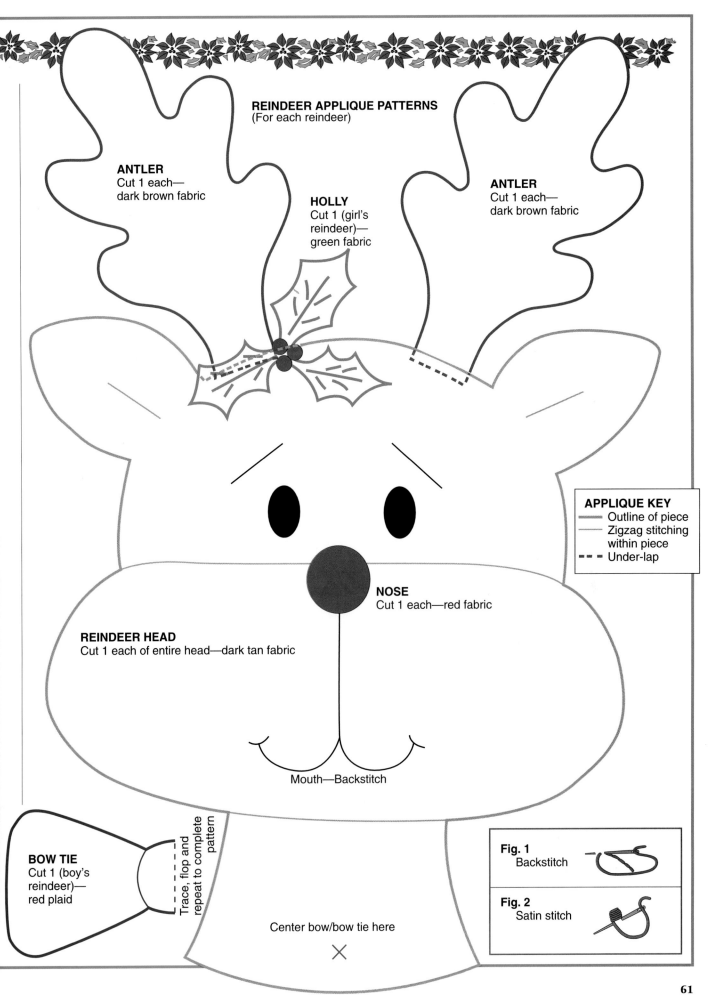

REINDEER APPLIQUE PATTERNS
(For each reindeer)

ANTLER
Cut 1 each—
dark brown fabric

HOLLY
Cut 1 (girl's
reindeer)—
green fabric

ANTLER
Cut 1 each—
dark brown fabric

APPLIQUE KEY
——— Outline of piece
——— Zigzag stitching
within piece
- - - Under-lap

NOSE
Cut 1 each—red fabric

REINDEER HEAD
Cut 1 each of entire head—dark tan fabric

Mouth—Backstitch

BOW TIE
Cut 1 (boy's
reindeer)—
red plaid

Trace, flop and
repeat to complete
pattern

Center bow/bow tie here

✕

Fig. 1
Backstitch

Fig. 2
Satin stitch

Craft Section...
Fixture Is Festive and Functional

SUGAR AND SPICE make the holidays nice, and this plastic canvas table caddy assures they're always in reach.

Shirley Wiskow of Jackson, New Jersey devised the Christmasy container for the dinner table. With compartments for salt, pepper, sugar packets and napkins, it's both pretty and practical for a season full of seasoning!

Materials Needed:
Charts on this page and the next page
One sheet of 7-mesh plastic canvas
Two 2-3/4-inch-long pieces of 18-gauge wire
Plastic canvas or worsted-weight yarn—60 yards of white, 15 yards of green, 1/2 yard of red and 1/3 yard of yellow*
Tapestry needle
Scissors
Plastic canvas cutter or sharp craft scissors
*Shirley used Nylon Plus yarn.

Finished Size: Table caddy measures 6-1/4 inches wide x 4 inches deep x 5 inches high.

Directions:
Referring to charts, cut out the pieces of the table caddy, remembering to cut pieces by counting the bars and not the holes. Also cut two 12-bar x 14-bar pieces for separators and two 13-bar x 15-bar pieces for sides.

Using tapestry needle and 18-in. lengths of yarn, follow charts and individual directions below to stitch pieces, referring to stitch illustrations in Fig. 1.

Work all pieces in Continental stitch, leaving unstitched the rows indicated on charts for separators and center upright joining lines.

For front, stitch wreath and holly designs with colors indicated on chart, then fill in the remainder of piece with white, leaving all joining lines unstitched.

Fill in the two separators, side pieces and base in white stitches, leaving all joining lines unstitched.

Fill in top of the center upright with green as shown on chart. Overcast edges of this section with green. Fill in rest of center upright with white, leaving all joining lines unstitched.

Fill in top of back upright with green as shown on chart. Overcast all edges of this section with green. Fill in rest of back upright with white, leaving all joining lines unstitched.

ASSEMBLY: Assembling as shown in Fig. 2 with right side of pieces out and right side of center upright toward the front, join a short edge of the two separators to the front piece, being careful to align the pieces along the bottom edges and making stitches to match the remaining stitches of the front.

Join side and front pieces to base, whipstitching edges together. Add center upright to base as directed for separators.

Whipstitch vertical edges of front and center upright to side pieces. Stitch the lower edges of the separators to base.

Overcast with white around the top edges of the center upright, front, sides and separators. Whipstitch back to base.

Bend wires as shown in Fig. 2. Place bent wires along the base and sides of the back as in Fig. 2. Overcast all remaining edges, stitching over wires and canvas at both back corners. ❈

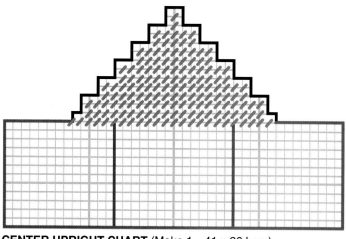

CENTER UPRIGHT CHART (Make 1—41 x 26 bars)

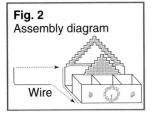

Fig. 1

Continental stitch

Overcast and whipstitch

FRONT CHART (Make 1—41 x 13 bars)

Fig. 2
Assembly diagram

Wire

COLOR KEY
- Red   — Joining lines
- Green   — Separator joining lines
- Yellow   — Center upright joining line

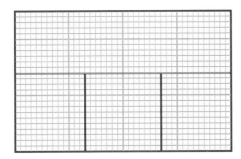

BASE CHART (Make 1—26 x 41 bars)

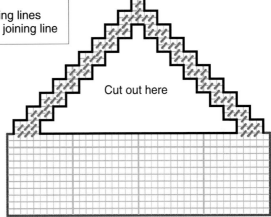

Cut out here

BACK UPRIGHT CHART (Make 1—41 x 33 bars)

These Spools Wind up as Bright Ideas

IN A FLASH…according to the creator of these spool candle holders—Rebecca Allison of Lexington, Ohio—that's how fast they come together. "They're easy gifts for kids to craft," she adds, "and they make a merry sight wherever you display them."

Materials Needed (for each one):
One 2-inch-tall wooden spool with thread removed
One candle (3-1/2 to 4 inches tall x 1/4 inch wide, for decorative use only)
Scrap of print fabric or wide ribbon
Scissors
Tacky (white) glue and/or glue gun and glue sticks
Desired decorations—dried flowers, tiny pinecones, tiny silk or plastic holly leaves or small gold jingle bells
12 inches of 1/8-inch-wide to 1/4-inch-wide satin or curling ribbon in green, gold or color of choice

Finished Size: Candle holder is about 2 inches tall plus candle.

Directions:
Measure the distance between the top and bottom rim of the spool and the distance around the spool plus a 1/2-in. overlap. Cut a strip of fabric or ribbon to this measurement.

Place a thin line of glue from top to bottom rim of spool and press one end of the fabric or ribbon onto spool. Wrap the ribbon or fabric strip around the spool and overlap the ends, adding glue as necessary to secure.

Glue about 1/2 in. of candle into top hole of the spool.

Arrange and glue small sprigs of dried flowers, holly leaves, pinecones or bells around the base of the candle as desired.

Tie a 12-in. length of ribbon around the base of the candle, finishing with a bow or curling ribbon ends. ❁

Table Runner's a Stocking Step Ahead

IN A HURRY? Don't worry...the feet in this stocking-stuffer stocking project are plenty fleet!

"My table runner stitches up quick, especially if your sewing machine will make blanket stitches," assures designer Jeanne Prue of Newport, Vermont.

Materials Needed:
Patterns on next page
1/4 yard of paper-backed fusible web
3/8 yard of tear-away stabilizer
100% cotton fabrics—3/8 yard each of dark green print and red solid, 1/2 yard of white/red print, 1/4 yard of white/green print, 1/4 yard of green plaid, 5/8 yard of muslin, 1/8 yard of white weaver's or kettle cloth and scraps in a variety of small Christmas prints
Matching thread
5/8 yard of 44-inch-wide fusible fleece
Black thread or embroidery floss (optional)
Embroidery needle (optional)
Invisible monofilament thread
Safety pins (optional)
Pencil
Quilter's ruler
Rotary cutter and cutting mat (optional)
Standard sewing supplies
Iron and ironing surface

Finished Size: Table runner measures 20 inches x 36 inches.

Directions:
Pre-wash fabrics without fabric softeners, washing colors separately. If the water from the fabrics is discolored, wash again until rinse water runs clear. Dry and press all fabrics.

CUTTING: Cut squares and strips using rotary cutter and quilter's ruler or scissors, cutting strips crosswise from selvage to selvage.

Cut these 5-1/4-in. squares: From dark green print, cut four squares. From red solid, cut 11 squares. From white/red print, cut seven squares. Cut each of these 5-1/4-in. squares diagonally into quarter-square triangles (Fig. 1).

From white/red print, cut two 4-7/8-in. squares. Cut each diagonally to make half-square triangles (Fig. 2) for outer corners of runner.

Cut these 4-1/2-in. squares: From white/red print, cut 11 squares. From white/green print, cut four squares. From green plaid, cut four squares.

From dark green print, cut three 2-1/4-in. x 44-in. strips for binding.

APPLIQUES: Trace individual applique pattern pieces 12 times onto the paper side of paper-backed fusible web, including under-laps to stocking as in-

dicated by the dashed lines on the pattern. The pattern is reversed to allow for correct placement after tracing and fusing steps are completed. Cut apart all shapes, leaving a 1/4-in. margin around each piece.

Fuse shapes to wrong side of each appropriate fabric following manufacturer's directions. *(Jeanne used red prints for each toe and heel of green print stockings and green prints for each toe and heel of red print stockings.)*

Cut out the fused fabric pieces and peel off paper backing.

Assemble stocking appliques and center on 4-1/2-in. squares as follows: place one each on four white/red print, four green plaid and four white/green print. Fuse stocking appliques in place.

Using two strands of black embroidery floss, blanket-stitch (Fig. 3) around each piece in this order: inner edge of toe, inner edge of heel, outer edge of stocking and outer edge of cuff. Or place tear-away stabilizer on wrong side behind applique pieces and machine satin-stitch or blanket-stitch the edges using matching or black thread.

ASSEMBLY: Do all piecing with accurate 1/4-in. seams and right sides of fabric together. Press seams toward darker fabric when possible.

Noting direction of the stocking ap-

pliques, lay out all pieces according to the Assembly Diagram (Fig. 4). Stitch together all quarter-square triangles to make 4-1/2-in. squares, carefully matching points of triangles. Then stitch all squares together to make rows (end rows will have a white/red print half-square triangle at each end). Stitch rows together to make the runner top, carefully matching corners of blocks.

Cut fusible fleece and muslin the same size as runner top. Fuse fleece to wrong side of top. Smooth backing out, wrong side up on a flat surface. Place top with fused fleece over backing, fleece side down, smoothing out layers. Pin or baste layers together about every 4 in., avoiding seams.

Using invisible thread on top and off-white thread in the bobbin, stitch-in-the-ditch of all rows vertically and horizontally, working from the center out, removing safety pins if needed. Machine baste around outer edges. Remove remaining safety pins or basting stitches.

BINDING: Stitch the short ends of the three 2-1/4-in. strips together to make one long strip. Fold in half lengthwise, wrong sides together, and press. Pin to right side of runner top, matching raw edges, beginning with a 1/4-in. fold to the wrong side. Stitch in a 1/4-in. seam, mitering corners. Overlap binding ends and trim away excess. Turn and pin binding to wrong side, mitering corners and covering the stitching.

Stitch-in-the-ditch of the binding from the top side, using invisible thread on top and thread to match the binding in the bobbin, carefully catching the folded edge of the binding underneath. Or hand-stitch binding to back. ❀

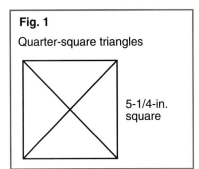

Fig. 1
Quarter-square triangles

5-1/4-in. square

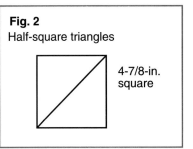

Fig. 2
Half-square triangles

4-7/8-in. square

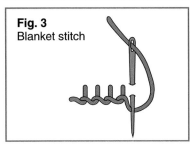

Fig. 3
Blanket stitch

STOCKING APPLIQUE PATTERNS
Trace 12 (each piece)—paper-backed fusible web

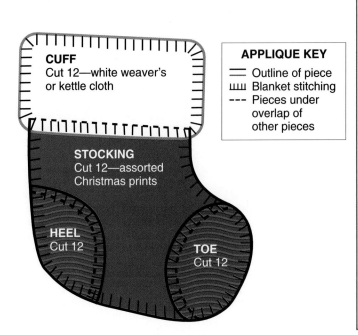

CUFF
Cut 12—white weaver's or kettle cloth

STOCKING
Cut 12—assorted Christmas prints

HEEL
Cut 12

TOE
Cut 12

APPLIQUE KEY
— Outline of piece
ⅢⅢ Blanket stitching
--- Pieces under overlap of other pieces

Fig. 4
Assembly diagram

FABRIC KEY
▨ Dark green print
▨ White/red print
▨ White/green print
▨ Green plaid
▨ Red solid

Calico Wreath Wraps up Fast

CELEBRATE the season in a rapidly roundabout way...with this simply sewn wreath. Loretta Kemna of St. Elizabeth, Missouri says the fabric stitches up in a matter of minutes. Then just add a bow, some holly and a couple of bears or deer (or other little figurines) so it all hangs together.

Materials Needed:
Patterns on next page
Tracing paper
Pencil
100% cotton fabrics—1/2 yard of dark green solid and 1/4 yard each of green print, red print, light-colored print and red solid
Matching thread
Standard sewing supplies
Polyester fiberfill
Pinking shears
Glue gun and glue sticks

Three red 3/4-inch pom-poms
Two small bears, deer or other light-weight holiday figurines
One 3/4-inch curtain ring

Finished Size: Wreath is 10 inches across x 14-1/2 inches tall, with bow.

Directions:
Trace one wedge pattern and four leaf patterns onto tracing paper and cut out.
WREATH: Pieced top: Cut fabrics as directed on wedge pattern. Do all stitching with right sides together and 1/4-in. seams. Press seams toward the darker fabric.

Sew one light-print wedge piece to a red-print wedge piece, stitching along one straight edge and backstitching at the beginning and end of each seam.

In the same way, add a green-print wedge piece to the opposite side of the light-print piece.

Alternating the colors as shown in

photo at left, continue adding wedge pieces, leaving the final seam open.

Backing: With right side up, smooth out a single layer of dark green solid fabric. Place the pieced wreath, wrong side up, on top and pin in place, arranging the raw edges of the open ends of pieced wreath so they touch as shown in Fig. 1.

Using the pieced wreath as your pattern, cut the dark green fabric along the outside edge of pieced wreath and along the open edges of wedge pieces. Cut out the center circle. Leaving pieces pinned, press under 1/4 in. along open wedge pieces and backing.

Stitch pieced wreath to backing around the entire outer edge, catching 1/4-in. folds in seam as shown in Fig. 2. In the same way, stitch around the entire inside circle. Clip curves, turn wreath right side out and press. Firmly stuff wreath and hand-stitch opening closed.

HOLLY LEAVES: With wrong sides together, fold remaining dark green solid fabric in half. Pin leaf patterns onto folded fabric. Leave at least 3/4 in. between pattern pieces.

Leaving the straight end of each leaf open for stuffing and using a straight stitch and matching thread, machine-stitch around each holly leaf, with the needle placed right next to edge of paper pattern. Remove patterns. Cut out leaves with pinking shears, adding a 1/4-in. seam allowance.

Leaving pieces unturned, stuff each leaf. Straight-stitch on center stitching line as shown on pattern.

Arrange leaves as shown in photo at left. Hot-glue leaves in place.

BOW: From red solid fabric, cut a 32-in. x 6-in. strip. With right sides together, fold strip in half lengthwise. Along the 32-in. length, measure 14 in. from each end and mark with a pin. There should be a 4-in. space between the two pins in the center of the long edge.

Leaving space between pins open for turning and using a 1/4-in. seam allowance, sew strip together along both short ends and the long edge.

Clip corners and turn bow right side out through opening. Turn in raw edges of opening and press bow. Hand-stitch opening closed. Tie a bow.

FINISHING: Hot-glue bow in center of holly leaves, covering the area where leaves come together.

For holly berries, glue a cluster of pom-poms over center of leaves. Glue bears, deer or other holiday figurines above pom-poms in center of wreath.

To hang wreath, hand-stitch a curtain ring in back at center top of wreath. ❈

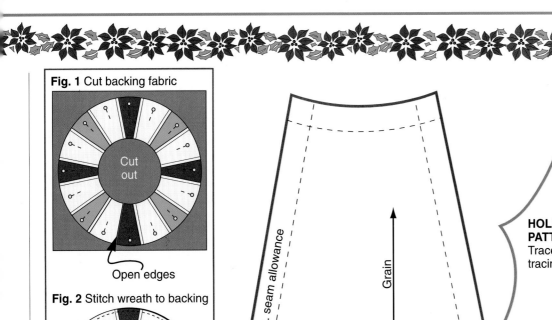

Fig. 1 Cut backing fabric

Cut out

Open edges

Fig. 2 Stitch wreath to backing

Leave open

1/4-in. seam allowance

Grain

WEDGE PATTERN
Cut 4—red print
Cut 4—green print
Cut 8—light print

HOLLY LEAF PATTERN
Trace 4—
tracing paper

Center stitching line

Grain

Plush Pillow Is Perky Plus

GIVE YOUR davenport a splash of Christmas this year...with a colorful pillow you can finish in a flash.

Country crafter Louise Purpura of Valparaiso, Indiana suggests decorating the center of the pillow with a bright holiday button, Christmas jewelry pin or a big cluster of shiny beads to make your sofa sparkle for the season.

Materials Needed:
Worsted-weight yarn in 4-ounce skeins—one skein each of red and green
Size 10-1/2 (7mm) straight knitting needles or size needed to obtain correct gauge
Scissors
Tapestry needle
12-inch pillow form

Gauge: In St st (knit 1 row, purl 1 row), 7 sts and 10 rows = 2 inches. To save time, take time to check gauge.

Finished Size: Pillow is about 12 inches square.

Knitting Reminder:
CHANGING COLORS: When changing from one color to another, twist one yarn around the other to join the two blocks.

Directions:
PILLOW FRONT/BACK: With green, cast on 50 sts.

Rows 1-4: Knit each row.

Row 5: With green, k 24, sl 1, drop green; pick up red, k 25.

Row 6: With red, p 24, sl 1, drop red; pick up green, p 25.

Rows 7-30: Repeat Rows 5-6.

Row 31: With red, k 24, sl 1, drop red; pick up green, k 25.

Row 32: With green, p 24, sl 1, drop green; pick up red, p 25.

Rows 33-56: Repeat Rows 31-32.

Rows 57-64: With red, knit.

Rows 65-116: Repeat Rows 5-56.

Rows 117-120: With green, knit each row. Bind off.

Fold pillow in half crosswise, right sides together. Stitch side edges together, leaving bottom edge open. Turn right side out and insert pillow form. Bring edges together and stitch closed. ❧

ABBREVIATIONS	
k	knit
p	purl
sl	slip
st(s)	stitch(es)

Santa's a Gourd-Looking Guy in Farm Wife's Eyes!

WHAT SHAPE is Santa Claus in? At Sharon Croy's, it all depends on how harvest has been.

"Every spring," the Marion, Missouri farm wife relates from the land where she and her husband raised two children, "Jerry and I plant an acre of gourds in our fertile sandy-loam soil. Later, with my paintbrush, I give them a personality all their own—Santa's.

"Santas made from bottle gourds have round heads, skinny necks and pudgy bodies. Ornamental gourds are more pear-shaped, so those Santas turn out short and squat."

Sharon's been using acrylic paint to provide gourds with a new guise since she was a girl. She learned from her father, who also liked to give them an expressive look.

Santa is her favorite, though, by far. In fact, he can be found year-round at the farm—especially in the loft of the Old Barn Gift Shop. The holiday items on its shelves are never out of season.

A few of her Santa gourds are large enough to become table centerpieces. Others star as earrings and pendants. Some even hang conveniently on a hook with their long curved stems.

The "Rattle Tattle Santa" has a cloth body and gourd head. "After the gourd has been dried," Sharon notes, "I put the seeds back in to give it the rattle."

Whatever type they are, her Santas take time to grow into the role. Sharon stores her harvested gourds for up to a year in a large shed to let them "cure", or dry out. Jerry's mother, Ada, helps by washing each gourd by hand.

In addition to the orb enterprise, the Croys grow pumpkins, squash and over 2,000 chrysanthemums on their farm, located not far from the historic Lewis and Clark Trail. They also whip up a wonderful dish of sliced apples, caramel and nuts for hungry visitors at the Feed Trough Snack Shop.

With all that on her agenda, Sharon is often pressed to get to her gourds. "I just fit in my Santas wherever I can," she says, "10 minutes here, 10 minutes there."

A Christmas rush? Sure. But that's something this country Claus creator gladly faces…365 days a year!

Editor's Note: *Croy's River Hills Farm is open 10 a.m.-4 p.m. Tuesdays through Saturdays and is located 2-1/2 miles northwest of Marion, Missouri on Highway 179. The phone number is 1-573/584-9653.* ❁

HO-HO-HOMEGROWN St. Nicks crop up in Sharon Croy's vegetable patch and in her fertile imagination. She draws jolly "Santa Squash" out of his shell (top) to shake up holiday decorating.

Christmas Cookie Maker Wings It—and Fans Flock

THE BILL of fare Kris Basta and family dish up for the holidays in rural Manhattan, Montana is a feast for the eyes …and beaks besides.

"You could say what we do is strictly for the birds," Kris observes. She, husband Ray, brother Marc Pierce and sister-in-law Sherrie produce a tweet treat—cookies made of birdseed.

The avian eatables actually come in 40 year-round designs. At Christmastime, though, the kitchen's aflutter with snowmen, bells, angels, candy canes and wreaths cut out to dispense season's feedings.

"I've designed a wooden base for each cookie, which we glaze with an edible adhesive and dip in a mix of wild birdseed," Kris explains. "Next, the piece is drilled to hold a dowel perch and twine hanger. Or, for a ground feeder, we attach a stake."

Waiting in the wings to supply appetizing ingredients are farmers from both Montana and North Dakota. "Local growers provide a wonderful seed variety—white and red millet, black thistle and sunflower seeds," Kris says.

"We like to use an assortment. That way, the feeders are colorful and attract different species." Indeed, the bird's-eye view through Kris' kitchen window features sparrow, dove, chickadee, finch and even woodpecker "gourmets" dropping in.

"What makes these ornaments extra-special is that our cookies are 'all-you-can-eat'," Kris grins. "When the original feed is gone, you can spread peanut butter or honey on the base and cover it with your own birdseed."

As for Kris' nest, the Bastas' young ones are active parts of the operation. "Our son, Eric, 14, is our right-hand assistant," his mother relates. "Daughter Dailey, 3, is a fledgling seed dipper.

"Traditionally, our families gather at holiday time and deck our backyard spruce with birdseed cookies," Kris continues. "Later on, we watch our 'dinner guests' flit between the branches—and listen as the tree bursts into song."

Editor's Note: *For a brochure and price list on Kris' birdseed cookies, write to Singing Tree Farms, P.O. Box 387, 110B S. Broadway, Manhattan MT 59741. Or dial 1-800/281-4745 (in the U.S.) or 1-406/284-6208 (in Canada).*

SEEDS-ONAL GOODIES Kris Basta, daughter (above left) create spread Christmas "chirps" across the country. Orders from birders keep Kris, rural neighbors busy making beak-pleasing feeders.

I'll Never Forget...

Lost Doll Found the Key to Love For a Lonely Little Girl

By Maggie Baxter of Ozark, Missouri

Standing in front of the Nativity at church that Christmas Eve many years ago, I whispered a desperate request. "Baby Jesus," my lips pleaded, "I won't ask for anything else—if You'll *please* send Mary Rose back to me."

Little did I know my prayer would be answered...in a way that touches me to this day.

I'm a grandmother myself now. Then, however, I was a little girl who—after my father had died and my mother had become ill—was growing up in the care of my grandmother.

Mary Rose? She was my very best friend—a beautiful doll with a porcelain face, golden curls and blue glass eyes that opened and closed.

Times were hard then. And, at her age, finding herself unexpectedly raising a child wasn't easy on Gram. So, even as young as I was, I'd understood her frustration when I'd received Mary Rose as a gift the previous Christmas.

"Totally impractical for a child on a farm," I had heard Gram mutter. "Shoes are what's needed!"

Now, almost a year later, it looked like Gram might have been right—*Mary Rose was missing*.

Retracing my steps, I remembered putting my doll down when I'd gone to open the gate for the cows. I was away for only a few minutes. But, in that short time, she'd disappeared. No matter how many times I recrossed the field's frozen ruts, there was no sign of her anywhere.

As Christmas neared, I almost dreaded the approaching celebration. Coloring holiday pictures and singing carols at school made my heart ache all the more for my Mary Rose.

On Christmas Eve night, Gram and I returned from church. Dispirited, I turned toward my dark bedroom.

"Wait, child," Gram directed, an unfamiliar quiver in her voice. "I have something for you." Seconds later, she was holding out a large box.

I opened it...and gasped in surprise. Inside, prettier than ever, was nestled Mary Rose!

In place of her tattered pink smock, she wore a bright red flowered dress. Her dingy bonnet had been starched and ironed. A white knitted coat and muff matched the tiny booties on her petite feet.

"You didn't lose her, child," Gram explained in a soft soothing tone. "I knew she was starting to look shabby. So I picked your doll up where you left her that day and decided to fix her up a bit."

Gram didn't stop there. Her hands on my shoulders, she assured me that, someday, my mother and I would be reunited. When that happened, Gram promised, I'd enjoy Christmases which were even more joyous.

She was right. Later, the Yuletide my son was born, the miracle of my first granddaughter...those, too, were days of unmatchable happiness.

The return of Mary Rose, though— and the door to Gram's deep love for me that doll opened—still warms my heart each holiday season. Merry Christmas!

Grandma's 'Brag' Page

GRIN AND BEAR IT...Cherubic Carter David Webster could've been forgiven if he hibernated through his first holidays, thanks to the warm fuzzies he found himself surrounded with. Grandma Judy Rice of Lapeer, Michigan shared the picture.

WRAPPED UP in the present time, precious Morgan Marinin proves that the very best things come in small packages, attests Grandma Mary Neisius, Prairie du Chien, Wisconsin.

CLAUS-KNIT. "Seeing my husband, Klaus, with our grandchildren—Nicolas, Chloe and Mikayla—is my Christmas wish come true," writes Lilo Gruenbeck of Costa Mesa, California.

HOWLIDAY SPIRIT reached full furry when her great-grandson and his pooch of a pal paused to pose at Noel, notes Audrey Christensen of Canby, Minnesota. "His parents love to dress up Trenton and his pup to fit the occasion," Audrey relates.

BETTER WATCH OUT. In a wink, Matthew Gardner appears to have a Nick knack, pens Grandma Gloria Pilkerton from Cleveland, Missouri.

SUITS HER FINE. Yuletide obviously sits right with bundled-up bundle-of-joy great-granddaughter Morgan Reynolds, remarks Goldie Creese of Grand Junction, Colorado.

Season Is in Full Bloom with Petal-Perfect Doily

RAISE this fanciful poinsettia for your holiday decor…then watch smiles crop up whenever folks enter the room.

But don't confine the design. Spread it around by giving doilies to special friends and relatives, advises crafter Emma Willey of Winston, Oregon.

Materials needed:
Size 10 crochet cotton—one ball each of red, white and green*
Size 4 (2mm) steel crochet hook
Tapestry needle
Scissors
*Emma used Knit-Cro-Sheen red and South Maid white and green.

Finished Size: Doily is 17 inches across.

Gauge: Round 1 = 3-1/2 inches across (tip of one petal to tip of opposite petal).

Special Abbreviations:
V-STITCH (V-st): Dc, ch 2, dc.
2 TREBLE CROCHET CLUSTER (2Tr-Cl): Yo twice, insert hk in the same or next sp as indicated in that round, draw up a lp, (yo, draw through 2 lps) twice, * yo twice, insert hk in same sp, draw up a lp, (yo, draw through 2 lps) twice *, yo, draw through remaining lps on hk.
3 TREBLE CROCHET CLUSTER (3Tr-Cl): Repeat 2TrCl, working sts between *'s one more time, then draw through all lps on hk.
4 TREBLE CROCHET CLUSTER (4Tr-

Cl): Repeat 2TrCl, working sts between *'s two more times, then draw through all lps on hk.
5 TREBLE CROCHET CLUSTER (5TrCl): Repeat 2TrCl, working sts between *'s three more times, then draw through all lps on hk.
2 DOUBLE TREBLE CROCHET CLUSTER (2DtrCl): Yo three times, insert hk in next sp, draw up a lp, (yo, draw through 2 lps) three times, * yo three times, insert hk in same st, draw up a lp, (yo, draw through 2 lps) three times *, yo, draw through remaining lps.
3 DOUBLE TREBLE CROCHET CLUSTER (3DtrCl): Repeat 2DtrCl, working sts between *'s one more time, then draw through all lps on hk.
2 TRIPLE TREBLE CROCHET CLUSTER (2trTrCl): * Yo four times, insert hk in same or next sp or st as indicated in that round, draw up a lp, (yo, draw through 2 lps) four times *, rep between *'s one more time, yo, draw through remaining lps on hk.
3 TRIPLE TREBLE CROCHET CLUSTER (3trTrCl): Repeat 2trTrCl between *'s three times, yo, draw through all lps on hk.

Directions:
With red, ch 6, join in first ch to form a ring. Work in rounds without turning

Round 1: Ch 1, * sc in ring, (ch 10, sc in second ch from hk, hdc in next ch, dc in next 5 ch, hdc in next ch, sc in last ch) for petal *, rep between *'s 11 times, end with sl st in beg sc: 12 petals formed. Fasten off red.

Round 2: Join white with sc in tip of any petal, * ch 6, sc in next petal tip *, rep between *'s 10 times, ch 6, end with sl st in beg sc.

Round 3: Ch 1, sc in same sc as sl st, * (hdc, 7 dc, hdc) in next ch-6 sp, sc in next sc *, rep between *'s 10 times, (hdc, 7 dc, hdc) in last ch-6 sp, end with sl st in beg sc. Fasten off white.

Round 4: Join green with sl st in any sc of Round 3 (at tip of petal); ch 5, (2trTrCl, ch 3, 3trTrCl) in same sc, * ch 7, sc in 4th dc of next 7-dc group, ch 7, (3trTrCl, ch 3, 3trTrCl) in next sc *, rep between *'s 10 times, ch 7, sc in 4th dc of last 7-dc group, ch 7, sl st in top of beg cl.

Round 5: Sl st into next ch-3 sp, ch 4, 2TrCl in same sp, * ch 7, 2TrCl over next two ch-7 sps (insert hk in first sp for first half of cl, then into second sp for second half of cl), ch 7, 3TrCl in next ch-3 sp *, rep between *'s around, ch 7, 2TrCl over next two ch-7 sps, ch 7, end with sl st in top of beg cl. Fasten off green.

Round 6: Join white with sl st in any 4th ch of any ch-7 sp, ch 5, dc in same st, * ch 7, V-st in 4th ch of next ch-7 sp *, rep between *'s around, ch 7, end with sl st in 3rd ch of beg ch-5.

Round 7: Sl st to 4th ch of next ch-7 sp, ch 5, dc in same st, * ch 7, V-st in 4th ch of next ch-7 *, rep between *'s around, ch 7, end with sl st in 3rd ch of beg ch-5.

Round 8: Rep Round 7.

Round 9: Ch 4 (counts as first tr), (2 tr, ch 1, 2 tr) in first ch-2 sp, tr in next dc, * ch 8, sc in ch-2 sp of next V-st, ch 8, tr in next dc, (2 tr, ch 1, 2 tr) in ch-2 sp of next V-st, tr in next dc *, rep between *'s around, ch 8, sc in ch-2 sp of next V-st, ch 8, end with sl st in top of beg ch-4: 6-tr groups form base of 12 "leaf" shapes around.

Round 10: Ch 4, tr in base of ch-4, tr in each of next 2 tr, ch 1, tr in each of next 2 tr, 2 tr in next tr, * (ch 5, sc in next sp) twice, ch 5, 2 tr in next tr, tr in each of next 2 tr, ch 1, tr in each of next 2 tr, 2 tr in next tr *, rep between *'s around, (ch 5, sc in next sp) twice, ch 5, end with sl st in top of beg ch-4.

Round 11: Ch 4, tr in each of next 3 tr, ch 1, tr in each of next 4 tr, * ch 5, sk next sp, (3DtrCl, ch 2, 3DtrCl, ch 2, 3DtrCl) in next sp, sk next sp, ch 5, tr in each of next 4 tr, ch 1, tr in each of next 4 tr *, rep between *'s around, ch 5, sk next sp, (3DtrCl, ch 2, 3DtrCl, ch 2, 3DtrCl) in next sp, sk next sp, ch 5, end with sl st in top of beg ch-4.

Round 12: Sl st in next tr, ch 4, tr in each of next 2 tr, ch 1, tr in each of next 3 tr, sk next tr, * ** ch 5, sc in next sp, ch 5, 3DtrCl in next ch-2 sp, ch 2, 3DtrCl in next ch-2 sp, ch 5, sc in next sp, ch 5, sk next tr **, tr in each of next 3 tr, ch 1, tr in each of next 3 tr *, rep between *'s around, rep between **'s one time, end with sl st in top of beg ch-4.

Round 13: Sl st in next 2 tr, [ch 4, 4TrCl in next ch-1 sp and next tr] for beg 5TrCl, * ** sk next 2 tr, (ch 5, sc in next sp) twice, ch 5, 3TrCl in next ch-2 sp, (ch 5, sc in next sp) twice, ch 5, sk next 2 tr **, 5TrCl in next tr, next ch-1 sp and following tr (to make 5TrCl, insert hk into next tr, then three times in next ch-1 sp

and once into following tr to complete) *, rep between *'s around, rep between **'s one time, end with sl st in top of beg cl: twelve 5TrCl and twelve 3TrCl.

Round 14: Sl st to center of next sp, sc in same sp, * ch 7, sc in next sp *, rep between *'s around, ch 7, end with sl st in top of beg sc: 72 sps.

Round 15: Sl st to center ch of next sp, ch 5, dc in same st, * ch 5, V-st in center ch of next sp *, rep between *'s around, ch 5, end with sl st in 3rd ch of beg ch.

Rounds 16 and 17: Rep Round 15. Fasten off white.

Round 18: Join red with sl st in ch-2 sp of any V-st, ch 5, dc in same st, * ch 2, sc in next sp, ch 2, V-st in ch-2 sp of next V-st *, rep between *'s around, end with ch 2, sc in next sp, ch 2, sl st in 3rd ch of beg ch-5. Fasten off. ❄

ABBREVIATIONS

beg	beginning	sc	single crochet
ch	chain	sk	skip
cl	cluster	sl	slip
dc	double crochet	sl st	slip stitch
hdc	half double crochet	sp(s)	space(s)
hk	hook	st(s)	stitch(es)
lp	loop	tr	treble crochet
rep	repeat	yo	yarn over

Beaded Pins Make Pretty Points

WEAR merry greetings on your coat or sweater with these pleasing pins from Renee Dent of Conrad, Montana.

The beaded beauties also find success at craft bazaars and as gifts. They are a hit wherever there's a lapel!

Materials Needed:
Charts on this page
Clear 14-count perforated plastic—one 1-1/2-inch x 3-1/2-inch piece for Noel pin and one 1-1/2-inch x 3-inch piece for Joy pin
White felt—one 1-1/2-inch x 3-1/2-inch piece for Noel pin and one 1-1/2-inch x 3-inch piece for Joy pin
Ecru six-strand embroidery floss
Seed beads—green, white, gold and red*

Size 26 tapestry needle
Scissors
Tacky glue
Two 1-inch bar pin backs

*Renee used Mill Hill seed beads, available at most craft stores. To find a store that carries the beads in your area, contact Mill Hill, P.O. Box 1060, Janesville WI 53547; 1-800/356-9438.

Finished Size: The Noel pin is 3/4 inch wide x 3-1/4 inches high; the design area is 12 beads wide x 42 beads high. The Joy pin is 3/4 inch wide x 2-3/8 inches high; the design area is 12 beads wide x 32 beads high.

Directions:
Cut a 36-in. piece of ecru six-strand floss and use one strand for all stitching.

Fold strand in half and thread both cut ends through needle.

Referring to chart, attach beads individually. To begin stitching, secure first bead with a half cross-stitch in upper left corner of perforated plastic, 1/2 in. from edge, as follows: From under perforated plastic, bring needle up through first hole

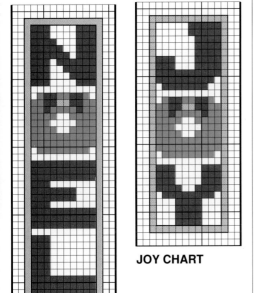

JOY CHART

NOEL CHART

BEADED PINS
COLOR KEY   Mill Hill Seed Beads
- Christmas Green 00167
- White 00479
- Gold 00557
- Red Red 02013

Fig. 1
Beaded half cross-stitch

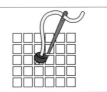

(the lower left of the stitch), allowing loop end of floss to extend out on wrong side. Pick up a bead with tip of needle, then go down into second hole (the upper right of the stitch) as in Fig. 1. As you do this, go through loop of floss underneath perforated plastic. Pull tightly.

Continue to add beads using half cross-stitches until pattern is complete. To end a strand and begin the next, run tails of floss under stitches on back.

When beading on design is completed, carefully trim away excess perforated plastic, leaving one bar outside of beaded stitching for whipstitching. Round off sharp corners.

Secure floss to remaining bar by following directions for securing first bead, making a stitch without adding a bead. Whipstitch edges, adding a gold bead with each stitch around entire design.

Glue design onto felt. When dry, trim away excess. Glue pin back to back 1/4 in. down from top edge. ❄

Craft Section...
Christmastime Critters Herd in Grins

HARNESSING holiday spirit by the sleighful is a breeze, thanks to this rollicking reindeer pair. They bring cheer wherever they appear!

Part of the deers' appeal lies in the soft flannels and felts that Amy Albert Bloom uses to construct them. "Those fabrics are fun to sew with," she details from Shillington, Pennsylvania. "Plus, they make the toys 'touchable'."

Materials Needed (for each reindeer):
Patterns on next page
Tracing or pattern paper
Transfer paper
Pencil
Tailor's chalk (optional)
1/4 yard or scraps of red plaid flannel or plain suede, felt, velour or pinwale corduroy fabric for reindeer body
Felt—9-inch x 12-inch piece of tan or white for antlers, ears and tail, scrap of black for nose and scraps of red, green and white for blanket and trim
15 inches of 1/4-inch-wide red or white rickrack
Polyester fiberfill
Fabric glue
Four pipe cleaners for antlers and legs
Two 4mm black seed beads for eyes
Pinking shears
Matching threads
Standard sewing supplies

Finished Size: Each reindeer is about 9 inches tall.

Directions:
Use a scant 1/4-in. seam with a small straight stitch, placing right sides together and backstitching at the beginning and end of each seam unless directed otherwise.

CUTTING: Trace patterns and all markings onto tracing or pattern paper and cut out. Cut out fabrics as directed on pattern pieces. Transfer markings.

REINDEER BODY: Stitch darts in each reindeer body piece where indicated on pattern.

Pin leg gusset to one reindeer body piece, carefully matching front, back and legs. Machine-stitch together, starting at neck edge (large dot) and stitching around front and back legs to back (large dot). Pin other reindeer body piece to leg gusset. Stitch, starting at the back edge and stitching around back and front legs to neck edge, stopping at same point as before. Trim seams and clip corners and curves.

Fold tail piece. With fold on top, pin tail to one body piece where indicated on pattern. Pin the two reindeer body pieces together and machine-stitch upper body seam, leaving opening for turning as indicated on pattern and starting and stopping at large dots on pattern. Trim seams and clip corners and curves. Turn reindeer right side out.

Stuff reindeer's legs firmly with polyester fiberfill.

Fold ends of pipe cleaner back about 2 in. Fold pipe cleaner into a U shape and push pipe cleaner down into stuffing of front legs. Repeat for back legs. Pipe cleaners will prevent the legs from splaying and help the reindeer to stand.

Stuff remainder of reindeer firmly.

Turn raw edges of opening to inside and hand-stitch opening closed.

ANTLERS: Place antler patterns on top of double layer of felt. Trace around patterns lightly with pencil or tailor's chalk. Remove patterns and machine-stitch along traced line through both layers of felt, leaving open at bottom where indicated. Trim close to stitching.

Fold ends of pipe cleaner back about 1/2 in. and insert pipe cleaner into antler between layers of felt as shown on pattern. Cut away excess pipe cleaner. Repeat for other antler.

At the points of each of the top darts on reindeer head, cut a slit into head just large enough for antlers to fit, where shown on pattern. Insert antlers and hand-stitch to head of reindeer.

FINISHING: Fold ears as indicated and hand-stitch in place over antlers as shown in photo. Hand-stitch nose to reindeer as shown in photo.

Hand-stitch beads in place for eyes where indicated on pattern, tugging gently on thread to indent beads slightly.

With pinking shears, cut a 2-1/2-in. x 5-3/4-in. piece of white or red felt for blanket and four green felt leaves. Cut two red or white felt berries with straight-edge scissors. Sew or glue leaves and berries to blanket as shown in photo. Add red or white rickrack trim to edge. Sew or glue blanket onto reindeer. ❈

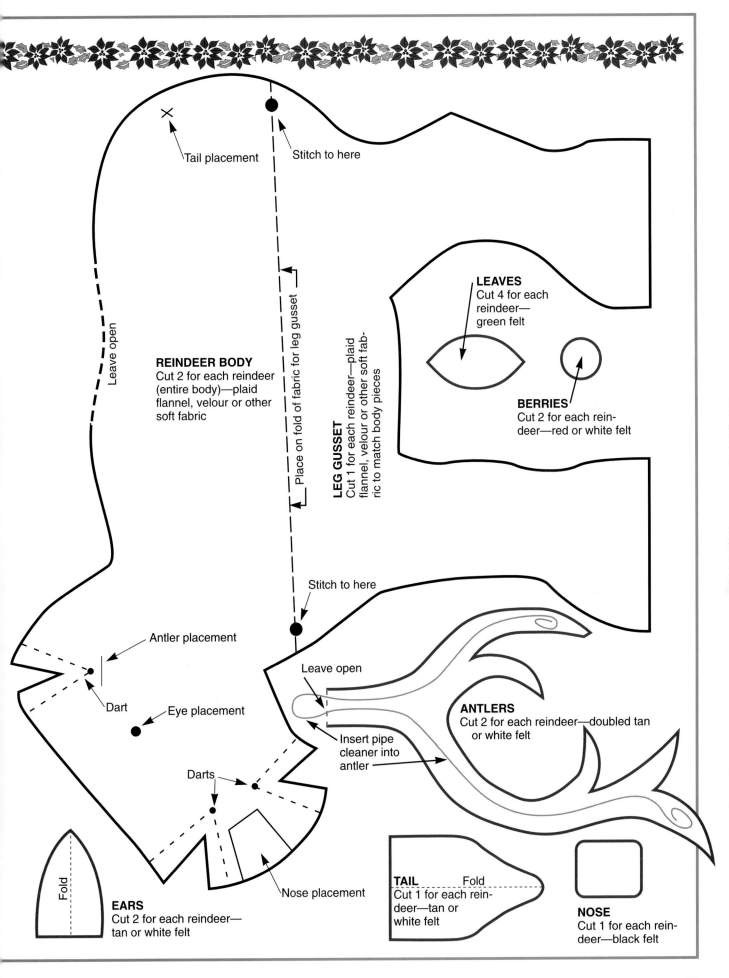

Tail placement

Stitch to here

Leave open

REINDEER BODY
Cut 2 for each reindeer
(entire body)—plaid
flannel, velour or other
soft fabric

Place on fold of fabric for leg gusset

LEG GUSSET
Cut 1 for each reindeer—plaid
flannel, velour or other soft fabric to match body pieces

LEAVES
Cut 4 for each
reindeer—
green felt

BERRIES
Cut 2 for each rein-
deer—red or white felt

Stitch to here

Antler placement

Dart

Eye placement

Leave open

Insert pipe
cleaner into
antler

ANTLERS
Cut 2 for each reindeer—doubled tan
or white felt

Darts

Nose placement

Fold

EARS
Cut 2 for each reindeer—
tan or white felt

TAIL   Fold
Cut 1 for each rein-
deer—tan or
white felt

NOSE
Cut 1 for each rein-
deer—black felt

Wooden Santa Stands for Glad Tidings

GOOD CHEER comes right to your doorstep when you add this spritely Santa to your December decor. With hands full of holiday happiness, he'll greet your guests with open arms, assures designer Patricia Schroedl of Jefferson, Wisconsin!

Materials Needed:

Patterns on pages 77 and 78
Transfer paper
Tracing paper and pencil
Stylus or dry ballpoint pen
Wood—14 inches of 1 x 8 pine for head, 6-1/4 inches of 1 x 6 pine for base, 3 feet of 1 x 4 pine for body (pine pieces are actually 3/4 inch thick), 2 feet of 2-inch-wide x 1/4-inch-thick wood for arms and 12-inch square of 1/4-inch plywood for birds and hearts
1/2-inch wooden furniture button/plug for nose
Band or scroll saw
Drill with 1/16-inch and 1/8-inch bits

Sandpaper
Tack cloth
Ruler
Stencil plastic or freezer paper
Fine-line permanent black marker
Craft (X-Acto) knife
Paints—white, flesh, red, forest green, brown, gray, black and metallic gold*
Snow texture paint*
Palette or paper plate
Paintbrushes—No. 8 flat, No. 4 round, No. 4 round scrubber, 1/2-inch stencil brush and 1-inch sponge brush
Toothpick (optional)
Spatter brush or old toothbrush
Paper towels
Newspapers
MinWax Wood Sheen stain and soft rag (optional)
Screwdriver
Drywall screws—two 2-inch, four 1-1/4-inch and three 3/4-inch
Needle-nose pliers
Two 6-inch pieces of 19-gauge black annealed wire
12-inch piece of 20-gauge gold wire
Wood glue
Six 5/8-inch gold jingle bells
6 feet of jute string
Spray varnish
Twelve 48-inch pieces of raffia

*Patricia used DecoArt Americana acrylic craft paints in Titanium White, Flesh Tone, Calico Red, Forest Green, Burnt Umber, Slate Gray, Lamp Black and Glorious Gold and DecoArt Snow-Tex to paint her Santa.

Finished Size: Santa is 24 inches wide x 46 inches high.

Directions:

Trace patterns on pages 77 and 78 onto tracing paper. Use transfer paper under patterns and stylus or dry ballpoint pen to transfer outlines of Santa head onto 1 x 8 pine, and hearts and birds onto plywood, matching grainlines.

Also, trace around mitten pattern on one end of the 24-in.-long wood arm piece. Reverse pattern and trace on the other end, making sure thumbs are along same edge.

Cut out each wood piece, using a band or scroll saw.

Drill holes as indicated on patterns into bottoms of birds and through top of Santa's head, each heart and both mittens. Also drill holes for birds through each end of arm piece, 1/2 in. from top (thumbs up) edge, making one hole 4 in.

from end of one mitten and the other 6-1/2 in. from end of opposite mitten.

Sand hearts, birds and base. Do not sand face, body or arms. Remove sanding dust with tack cloth.

PAINTING: Using the No. 8 flat brush for smaller areas and sponge brush for large areas, basecoat front and edges of cut wood pieces as follows: Basecoat beard, mustache and fur trim on Santa white; hat, arms (not mittens) and body red; mittens forest green; and face and 1/2-in. wood plug/button flesh.

Basecoat front of hearts white and edges metallic gold. Basecoat both sides of birds white. It may take more than one coat to cover each piece. Let dry between coats.

Stenciling: Trace stencil patterns (Noel letters, tree, holly leaves and ornament) onto stencil plastic or freezer paper with black marker and cut out areas with craft knife.

Position stencils on wood pieces and stencil as follows: Dip stencil brush in paint and wipe off on paper towel so it is almost dry. Hold brush perpendicular to piece and apply paint with up-and-down motion in cutout areas of stencils.

Use red paint to add a different letter to each heart. Use forest green to apply holly leaves to hearts as shown in photo at left and to apply green portion of tree to body and arms, making two treetop halves evenly spaced on each arm and seven complete trees randomly placed on body. To each tree, add a gold star on top and randomly placed gold ornaments as shown in photo. Add tree bases in brown.

Details: Paint the details freehand or transfer the pattern lines onto Santa head pieces and both sides of birds, using transfer paper.

Use gray and the No. 8 flat brush to shade along lines of beard and mustache and under curve of bird wings.

To shade, dip brush in clean water. Remove excess water by touching the brush to a paper towel until shine disappears. Gently touch one corner of the brush in paint and brush it back and forth on palette to blend paint into brush. Apply paint with the loaded edge of brush toward line marked on pattern.

Use handle of large brush and black to dot eyes on Santa and handle of medium brush and black to dot eyes on birds. Use handle of medium brush and red to dot holly berries on hearts.

Use round brush to add black mouth, red lips and white eyebrows.

Dip round scrubber in red paint and wipe off on paper towel until almost dry. Hold brush perpendicular to button/plug nose and cheeks and lightly apply paint with an up-and-down motion.

Use the sponge brush to apply snow texture paint to top of base and Santa's hatband.

Glue button/plug nose onto face where indicated on Santa head pattern.

Sand body, head and arms, wearing away edges and exposing some wood grain for an aged look.

Spattering: Place wood pieces on newspaper to protect surfaces around and underneath them.

Mix about 1/2 teaspoon of white paint with 1/2 teaspoon of water. Using an old toothbrush or spatter brush, dip brush into thinned paint. Hold bristles toward piece about 8 in. from area to be spattered and pull another brush handle or finger across bristles. *(Spattering may be easier to do outdoors.)* Let dry.

Finishing: If desired, stain unpainted areas of all pieces, wiping off excess stain with soft rag. Let dry.

Spray each piece with one or more coats of varnish, allowing drying time between coats.

ASSEMBLY: Screw base to body piece, centering bottom of body piece on top of base and inserting both 2-in. screws up through bottom of base.

Screw body piece to back of head piece, placing point of Santa's beard 5 in. below top edge of body piece and inserting 1-1/4-in. screws from back to front. Repeat to add arms to back of body, using 3/4-in. screws, positioning arms perpendicular to body with top edge of arms centered 3-1/2 in. from top edge of body piece and thumbs up.

Wires: Use needle-nose pliers to bend 1/2 in. of one end of each piece of black wire back on itself. Dip bent ends into wood glue and insert into drilled holes of birds. Let dry.

Referring to photo, attach birds as follows: Pull unbent end of one bird's wire through one of the bird holes in the arm piece, bringing it from front to back until bottom of bird is 3/4 in. above arm. Bend wire around to front over top of arm. Wrap remaining wire around brush handle to coil, bending coil tightly to arm. Repeat for second bird.

Insert gold wire through hole of Santa's hat, having ends extend evenly. Twist wire together once above hat. Add a jingle bell to each wire end. Twist wire again and wrap each end around brush handle to form coils.

Jute/Raffia: String Noel hearts onto jute piece, bringing jute from front to back through hole on one side of "N" heart, across back of heart, then from back to front through other hole. Leaving 2 in. of jute between hearts, attach remaining hearts, spelling "Noel" and centering hearts on jute piece.

Insert ends of jute through holes in mittens. Tie to mittens so 25 in. of garland hangs between mittens and jute ends are even.

Holding six strands of raffia together, make a 3-1/2-in. bow at center of strands. Use jute end to tie bow to one mitten. Repeat with remaining raffia.

Tie two jingle bells to each end of jute piece, knotting one 5-1/2 in. from mitten and the other 11 in. from mitten.

(Patterns continue on the next page)

HOLLY LEAVES STENCIL PATTERN
Trace 1 each—stencil plastic or freezer paper

NOEL STENCIL PATTERN
Trace 1 (each letter)—stencil plastic or freezer paper

Drill 1/8-in. hole here

Note: Trace mittens onto each end of 24-in.-long arm piece, reversing pattern for second mitten with thumbs up along same edge.

MITTEN ENDS (for arm piece)
Trace 2, reversing 1—1/4-in. wood

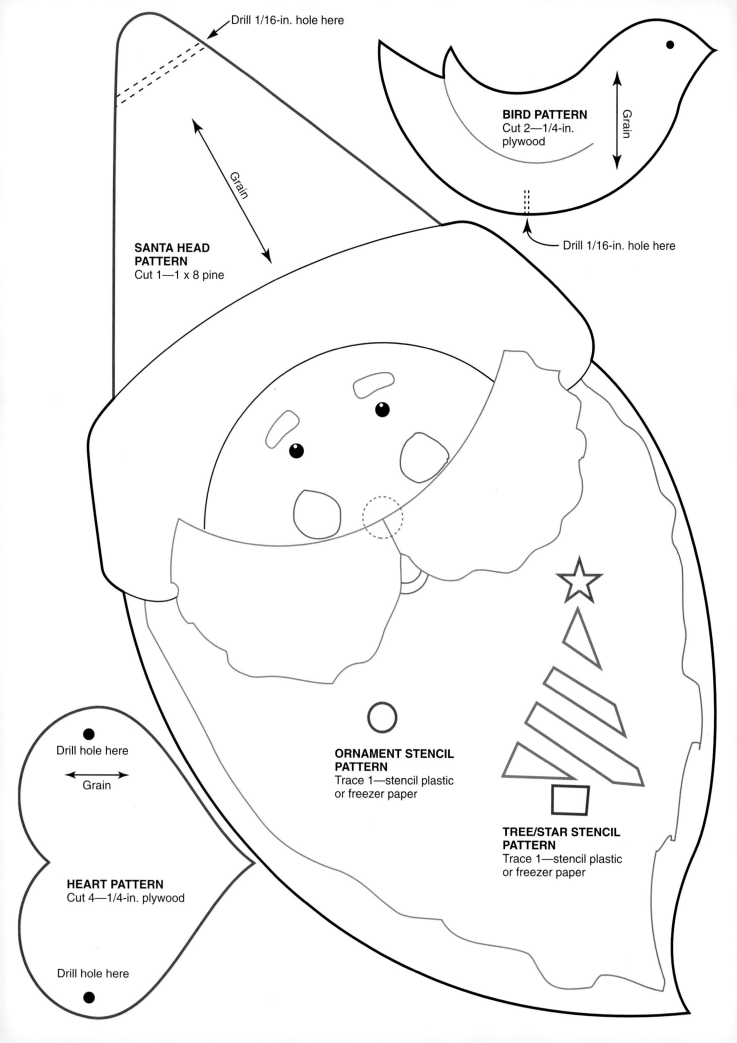

Drill 1/16-in. hole here

BIRD PATTERN
Cut 2—1/4-in.
plywood

Grain

Drill 1/16-in. hole here

Grain

SANTA HEAD PATTERN
Cut 1—1 x 8 pine

Drill hole here

Grain

HEART PATTERN
Cut 4—1/4-in. plywood

Drill hole here

ORNAMENT STENCIL PATTERN
Trace 1—stencil plastic or freezer paper

TREE/STAR STENCIL PATTERN
Trace 1—stencil plastic or freezer paper

Craft Section...
Holiday Hot Pad Makes the Rounds

ANY DISH will be all dressed up for Christmas with this handsome hot pad. It's been a longtime holiday favorite at Barbara McLeod-Pegg's home in Sunderland, Ontario. "The hot pad is a variation of a pattern my 87-year-old mother uses," she explains.

Materials Needed:
Size 10 crochet cotton—one 350-yard or 400-yard ball each of red, green and white*
Size 6 (1.75mm) steel crochet hook
Tapestry needle
Scissors
*Barbara used South Maid 100% mercerized crochet cotton.

Finished Size: Hot pad measures about 7 inches across.

Gauge: 8 dc = 1 inch.

Directions:
With red, ch 6; sl st in first ch to form a ring.

Rnd 1: Ch 3, work 11 dc in ring (12 dc). Join with sl st in top of ch-3. (The beg ch-3 always counts as 1 dc.)

Rnd 2: Ch 3, work 1 dc in same st as joining sl st; work 2 dc in each dc around (24 dc). Join with sl st in top of beg ch-3.

Rnd 3: Ch 3, work 2 dc in next dc; * work 1 dc in next dc, 2 dc in next dc; repeat from * around (36 dc). Join with sl st in top of beg ch-3. Fasten off red.

Rnd 4: Join white. Ch 3, work 1 dc in next dc, 2 dc in next dc; * work 1 dc in each of next 2 dc, 2 dc in next dc; repeat from * around, (48 dc). Join with sl st in top of beg ch-3.

Rnd 5: Ch 3, work 1 dc in each of next 2 dc, 2 dc in next dc; * work 1 dc in each of next 3 dc, 2 dc in next dc; repeat from * around (60 dc). Join with sl st in top of beg ch-3.

Rnd 6: Ch 3, work 1 dc in each of next 3 dc, 2 dc in next dc; * work 1 dc in each of next 4 dc, 2 dc in next dc; repeat from * around (72 dc). Join with sl st in top of beg ch-3. Fasten off white.

Rnd 7: Join green. Ch 3, work 1 dc in each of next 4 dc, 2 dc in next dc; * work 1 dc in each of next 5 dc, 2 dc in next dc; repeat from * around (84 dc). Join with sl st in top of beg ch-3.

Rnd 8: Ch 3, work 1 dc in each of next 5 dc, 2 dc in next dc; * work 1 dc in each of next 6 dc, 2 dc in next dc; repeat from * around (96 dc). Join with sl st in top of beg ch-3.

Rnd 9: Ch 3, work 1 dc in each of next 6 dc, 2 dc in next dc; * work 1 dc in each of next 7 dc, 2 dc in next dc; repeat from * around (108 dc). Join with sl st in top of beg ch-3. Fasten off.

Repeat Rnds 1-9 with white for a second piece. Use tapestry needle to weave in loose ends.

FINISHING: Place both pieces wrong sides together. With sections matching, attach white with a sl st through both pieces, ch 1, sc in same st as sl st.

EDGING: Rnd 1: Working each st through both pieces, work 1 sc in each of next 7 dc, work 2 sc in next dc; * work 1 sc in each of next 8 dc, work 2 sc in next dc; repeat from * around (120 sc). Join with sl st in ch-1 space.

Rnd 2: * Ch 6, skip next 4 sc and sl st in next sc; repeat from * around (24 loops). Join with sl st in same ch-1 space as Rnd 1.

Rnd 3: In first ch-6 space, work 1 sl st, ch 3, 6 dc, ch 1, 7 dc; in each remaining ch-6 loop work (7 dc, ch 1, 7 dc). Join with sl st in top of beg ch-3. Fasten off white.

Rnd 4: Join red in top of same ch-3 space as last sl st. Ch 3, work 1 dc in each dc to first ch-1 space; * in ch-1 space work (1 dc, ch 1, 1 dc), work 1 dc in each dc to next ch-1 space; repeat from * around ending with 1 dc in each dc to end. Join with sl st in top of ch-3. Fasten off red.

Rnd 5: With white, repeat Edging Rnd 4. Fasten off.

Rnd 6: With green, repeat Edging Rnd 4. Fasten off.

FINISHING: Use tapestry needle to weave in remaining loose ends. ❈

ABBREVIATIONS:	
beg	beginning
ch(s)	chain(s)
sc	single crochet
dc	double crochet
rnd	round
sl st	slip stitch
st(s)	stitch(es)

This North Pole Necktie Comes Frosted with Fun

INSTEAD of giving Dad a plain old tie for Christmas, pack it full of happy personality by painting this friendly snowman right onto it.

The technique is easy enough for just about anyone to try, assures crafter Verlyn King of Tremonton, Utah. She also notes that, when December's done, Dad can wear his new tie all the way through winter as well.

Materials Needed:

Pattern on this page
Tracing paper
Transfer paper
Pencil
Toothpick
Acrylic fabric paints (or regular acrylic craft paints plus textile medium)—white, black, orange, red, green and yellow
Dimensional fabric paint—white and iridescent white
Paintbrushes—No. 4 flat and fine liner
Green glitter and craft glue or green glitter fabric paint
Purchased necktie—navy with tiny white polka dots or navy solid
Paper plate or palette
Masking tape or straight pins
Scissors

Finished Size: The snowman design is about 7 inches tall and will fit on most neckties. The pattern can be enlarged or reduced on a copy machine to fit other types of garments as well.

Directions:

Knot tie in length it will be worn, then loosen to remove tie—but do not untie, as knot will be decorated.

Trace pattern onto tracing paper. Cut out.

PAINTING: Place a small amount of each color paint on paper plate or palette as needed. Allow paint to dry between each application.

Position pattern on right side of wide end of tie front with bottom edge of snowman about 1-3/4 in. from tip. Pin or tape in place.

Trace the outline of snowman and snow onto tie, using a toothpick dipped in white paint.

Paint snowman and snow white with flat brush, using a gentle scrubbing motion. Paint snow out to side edges of tie and tip as shown in photo at left.

Paint hat with flat brush and black, extending paint into white outline a bit.

When paints are thoroughly dry, place transfer paper over painted snowman and position snowman pattern on top, taking care to match previous outline. Trace over nose, eyes, mouth, buttons, scarf and detail lines on snow with pencil.

Using liner brush, paint nose orange. Paint yellow and green stripes in scarf and yellow in fringe. Let dry. Paint red lines in scarf and fringe.

Using black paint and liner brush, paint detail lines on snow, snowman and scarf. Then paint nose, eyes, buttons and mouth as indicated on pattern. Let dry.

Using liner brush, paint white zigzags in scarf and highlights on nose, eyes, buttons and mouth. Dip flat brush in white paint and remove excess until nearly dry; add highlights to crown of hat, as shown on pattern.

Place small dots of glue randomly on front and knot of tie, applying on polka dots if your tie has them, and sprinkle with glitter. Or paint dots using glitter fabric paint. Let dry.

Using flat brush, "rub" iridescent paint randomly on snowman and snow underneath. Use handle of paintbrush and iridescent paint to randomly dot several snowflakes on front of tie, again applying on polka dots if your tie has them.

Referring to photo, paint five snowflake designs on front of tie using white dimensional paint, placing smaller snowflakes near knot and adding random "snowflake dots" to front of tie and knot of tie. Dry flat for at least 4 hours.

Do not iron or launder. Use a damp sponge to clean if necessary. ❀

SNOWMAN PATTERN
Trace 1—tracing paper

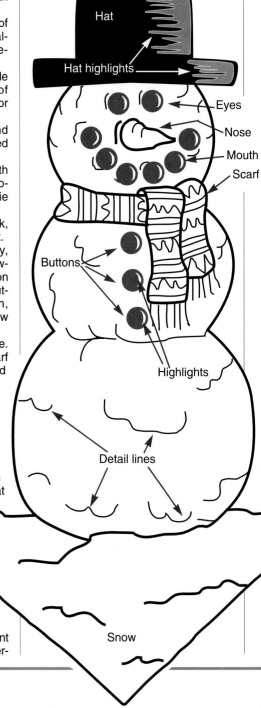

'Moorry' Magnet Makes an Easy Holiday Pleaser

FOR a bovine way to brighten your kitchen at Christmas, follow Bette Veinot's lead—just round up a Holstein magnet to beef up the refrigerator door.

Bette, who lives in Bridgewater, Nova Scotia, also notes that her cow makes a dandy dairy trim for the tree, too.

Materials Needed:

Patterns on this page
Tracing or pattern paper
Pencil
Compass
Cotton or cotton/polyester fabrics—5-inch x 8-inch scrap of white for cow body and head and scrap of dark green print for leaves
Scrap of tan felt for horns
Scrap of fusible web
Black acrylic craft or fabric paint
No. 4 flat paintbrush
Paper plate or palette
Plastic container top (coffee can or margarine lid)
Two 7mm movable glue-on eyes
One 6mm jingle bell
One 1/2-inch-wide beige button
Scrap of white plastic art foam for ears and hooves
One 1/4-inch red pom-pom
4 inches of jute string
Paper towels
Waxed paper
Masking tape
Glue gun and glue sticks or craft glue
White all-purpose thread
Hand-sewing needle
Fine-line permanent black marker
4 inches of 1/8-inch-wide metallic gold ribbon
Scissors
Measuring tape
1-inch flat magnetic strip
Iron and ironing surface

Finished Size: Cow is 3 inches across.

Directions:
Trace patterns onto tracing or pattern paper and cut out. Also, use compass to draw four circle patterns onto tracing or pattern paper, measuring 1-1/4 in., 2 in., 2-1/2 in. and 4 in. across. Cut out the four circle patterns.

Using fusible web, fuse wrong sides of two 1-1/2-in. squares of green print fabric together, following manufacturer's directions.

PAINTING: Place white fabric on waxed paper and tape in place.

Using patterns, trace one 4-in. circle for cow body and one 2-in. circle for cow head onto white fabric. Using flat paintbrush and black paint, paint random spots onto white fabric. To paint spots, begin in center and work outward, painting various shapes and sizes (see Fig. 1). Be sure to paint spots close to edges of circles. Let dry.

CUTTING: Cut 4-in. body circle and 2-1/2-in. head circle from painted "cow spots" fabric.

Place 2-1/2-in. circle pattern and 1-1/4-in. circle pattern on top of plastic lids and trace around each pattern once. Cut out along traced lines.

Trace two ears and two hooves, using tracing paper patterns, onto white plastic art foam and cut out.

Using horn pattern, cut two horns from tan felt. Using holly leaf pattern, cut two holly leaves from fused green Christmas print.

ASSEMBLY: Using a running stitch (Fig. 2), hand-stitch 1/4 in. from edge around outside of body, leaving long thread ends.

Place large plastic circle on wrong side of body piece 1/2 in. from right edge, and pull thread ends tight. Tie thread ends and clip close to knot. Smooth out wrinkles around outer edge of body piece and push opening as far to the right as possible.

Repeat, using head piece and small plastic circle. Center opening on cow head after fastening and clipping ends.

With white thread, hand-sew a couple of stitches through the button. Clip thread ends.

Draw broken lines around outside edges of ears and hooves as shown on patterns and in photo, using fine-line black marker.

Following Assembly Diagram (Fig. 3) for placement, glue ears and horns onto back (smooth side) of head and glue

hooves onto back (smooth side) of body. Let dry.

Place body smooth side down on flat surface and glue back of head, slightly off center, onto body. Glue eyes and button onto front (gathered side) of head. Let dry.

Tie metallic gold ribbon into small bow and glue bow to bottom of head. Trim ends as desired.

Glue bell just below ribbon bow.

Glue one end of jute string to back of cow body at top center. Untwist about 1 in. of other end of jute string to form end of tail and glue to front of cow body about 1 in. from end.

Glue holly leaves and pom-pom onto tail. Glue magnet onto center back. ✿

EAR PATTERN
Cut 2—
white plastic
art foam

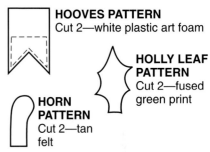

HOOVES PATTERN
Cut 2—white plastic art foam

HOLLY LEAF PATTERN
Cut 2—fused green print

HORN PATTERN
Cut 2—tan felt

Fig. 1 Painting "cow spots"

Fig. 2 Running Stitch

Fig. 3 Assembly Diagram
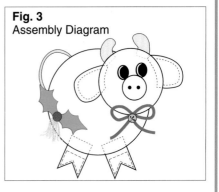

Angels on Walls Spotlight Important Part of Season

A FAST WAY to ensure the real meaning of Christmas stays in focus at your house are these quick-to-quilt wall hangings, which come from Linda Whitener of Glen Allen, Missouri. Follow her color suggestions…or feel free to choose those that work best with your own individual home decor.

Materials Needed (for each):
Applique patterns on next page
Pencil
36-inch-wide to 44-inch-wide 100% cotton fabrics—1/2 yard of muslin and 1/8 yard of print or plaid for border
Fabric scraps—gold solid and flesh solid and two to three assorted prints or plaids that coordinate and contrast with print or plaid border fabric (see note)
1/4 yard of paper-backed fusible web
15-inch square of bonded batting
Rotary cutter and cutting mat (optional)
Quilter's ruler
Water-soluble marker (optional)
Matching thread
Standard sewing supplies
Small amount of light brown yarn

Note: Refer to wall hangings in photo above to help you choose fabrics that work well together, or select from your own scrap fabrics for color and pattern combinations you prefer.

Finished Size: Wall hangings are 13-1/2 inches square.

Directions:
Do all piecing with accurate 1/4-in. seams and right sides of fabric together. Press seams toward darker fabrics when possible.

CUTTING: Cut squares and strips using rotary cutter and quilter's ruler, or mark strips with water-soluble marker and ruler, and use scissors to cut strips crosswise from selvage to selvage.

From muslin, cut one 11-in. square for applique background and one 15-in. square for backing.

For the border, cut four 2-in. x 11-in. strips from print or plaid.

For pieced corners, from a contrasting print scrap, cut one 1-1/4-in. x 11-in. strip. From muslin or coordinating print scrap, cut one 1-1/4-in. x 11-in. strip.

APPLIQUES: Omitting scarf (to be added later), trace individual pieces of applique patterns onto paper side of fusible web, including under-laps as indicated by dashed lines on pattern. Trace angel dress and wings each in one piece and trace three stars. Angel pattern is reversed to allow for correct placement after tracing and fusing steps. Cut apart all shapes, leaving a 1/2-in. margin around each piece.

Place fusible web shapes on wrong side of fabrics, using flesh solid for hands and head, gold solid for horn and contrasting prints or plaids for stars, wings and dress. Fuse in place following manufacturer's directions.

To transfer the inner wing line, use tan thread to straight-stitch along the line traced on the paper backing before removing it from the piece. Cut out fused fabrics along traced outlines. Peel paper backing off each piece.

Referring to applique pattern and photo for placement, position pieces on 11-in. muslin background square. Fuse in place.

PIECING: Corner Squares: Sew long edges of the 1-1/4-in. x 11-in. strips together. Press. Cut strip into eight pieces, each 1-1/4 in. long. See Fig. 1a. Press.

Sew pieces as shown in Fig. 1b to form four corner squares. Press.

Borders: Sew one 2-in. x 11-in. border strip on each side of the 11-in. muslin background square. Press.

Sew one corner square to each end of the remaining two 2-in. x 11-in. border strips, turning corner squares so the lighter color square will be toward the center of the wall hanging when attached. Sew these borders to the remaining edges of the background/borders, carefully matching corners. Press.

ASSEMBLY: Layer batting, 15-in. muslin backing square (right side up) and then pieced top (wrong side up). Pin layers together. Sew 1/4 in. from all outside edges of the pieced top, leaving a 4-in. opening on one edge for turning.

Trim seam even with outside edge of pieced top and clip corners close to stitching. Turn right side out. Pin opening closed and edgestitch around entire outside edge.

To quilt, stitch-in-the-ditch between border pieces, corner squares and muslin background square.

APPLIQUE STITCHING: Pin all layers together around applique to hold them in place when stitching. Using matching thread and medium-width satin zigzag setting on machine, applique in this order: horn, hand, dress, back wing, front wing, head and stars. Pull all thread ends to back of work and secure.

Angel's Scarf: Cut bias (45° angle) pieces of a contrasting print fabric, one

9 in. x 1 in. and one 5 in. x 1 in. Press under 1/4 in. on all long edges. Pin these on top of the angel, stretching and curving them to follow the pattern, overlapping the 9-in. piece over the 5-in. piece and folding ends in at an angle as shown on pattern. Edge-stitch all edges of each scarf piece.

ANGEL'S HAIR: Loop yarn 10 times around three fingers held together. Hold the "loops" of yarn open and machine-stitch loops to top of angel's head where indicated on pattern. Bring the loops down to hide the stitches and make a few small hand-stitches in the hair near the shoulders to keep hair in place.

FINISHING: Stitch thread loop centered at top edge of back for hanger. ❈

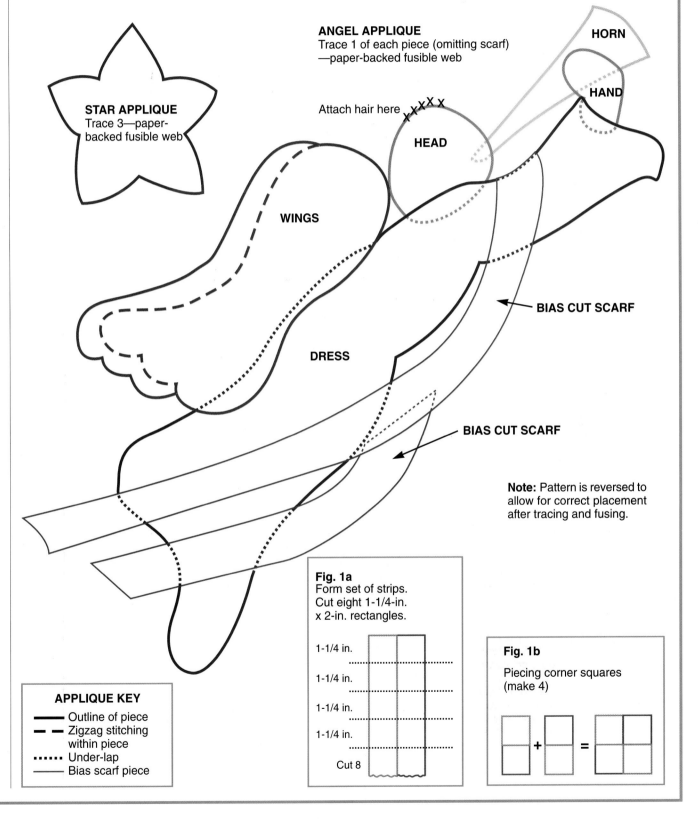

STAR APPLIQUE
Trace 3—paper-backed fusible web

ANGEL APPLIQUE
Trace 1 of each piece (omitting scarf)
—paper-backed fusible web

Attach hair here x x^x^X X x

HEAD

HORN

HAND

WINGS

DRESS

BIAS CUT SCARF

BIAS CUT SCARF

Note: Pattern is reversed to allow for correct placement after tracing and fusing.

Fig. 1a
Form set of strips.
Cut eight 1-1/4-in.
x 2-in. rectangles.

1-1/4 in.

1-1/4 in.

1-1/4 in.

1-1/4 in.

Cut 8

Fig. 1b

Piecing corner squares
(make 4)

☐ + ☐ = ☐

APPLIQUE KEY
— Outline of piece
– – Zigzag stitching within piece
••••• Under-lap
— Bias scarf piece

Craft Section...
Paint Puts Sweatshirt In Fine Festive Mood

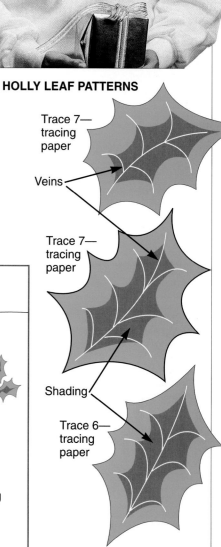

ALL a sweatshirt needs to improve its image for the holidays is...a paint job! Jean Devore of Jackson, Missouri crafted this jolly design that really shines. For extra sparkle, she highlighted the holly leaves with green glitter.

Materials Needed:
Patterns on this page
Tracing or pattern paper
Air-soluble or water-soluble marker
Pencil
White cotton/polyester blend sweatshirt
Acrylic fabric paints (or regular acrylic paints plus textile medium)—red, Kelly green, white and black
Green glitter paint
Paintbrushes—No. 4 flat and fine liner
Paper plate or palette
Paper towels
Round cabochons (flat-backed acrylic stones with a smooth domed top)— four 9mm red, one 9mm green, one 14mm red and one 14mm green
Clear, fast-drying fabric glue
T-shirt board or heavy cardboard to fit inside sweatshirt
Waxed paper
Scissors
Straight pins

Finished Size: Holly design is 12 inches x 16 inches and is shown painted on an Adult size Medium sweatshirt.

Directions:
Pre-wash and machine-dry sweatshirt. Do not use detergents that have built-in stain resistors or fabric softeners. Press if needed.

Trace holly patterns onto tracing or pattern paper as many times as directed on patterns and cut out.

Place a piece of waxed paper on T-shirt board or cardboard to protect surface. With right side out, slip T-shirt board or cardboard inside sweatshirt. Smooth sweatshirt and pin sleeves out of the way. Place on flat surface.

Arrange traced patterns on top of sweatshirt front. Group, overlap and reverse patterns as needed to create the design shown in Fig. 1. Pin in place and trace around patterns using air-soluble or water-soluble marker.

PAINTING: Place small amounts of each paint on paper plate or palette as needed. (If necessary, mix paints with textile medium prior to use.)

Using flat brush, paint each holly leaf Kelly green. When partially dry, shade the centers of leaves and areas that overlap as shown in the design diagram below.

To shade, dip flat brush in clean water. Remove excess water by touching the brush to a paper towel. Touch one corner of brush in black paint and brush it on waxed paper to blend paint into brush.

Apply the paint with loaded edge of brush in centers of leaves and edges of areas that overlap. Let dry.

Using flat brush, paint each holly berry red. Shade with black as directed for holly leaves. Let dry.

Using flat brush and a half-circle brush stroke, highlight each berry with white paint as shown in Fig. 1. Let dry.

Using liner and white paint, paint the veins in the holly leaves. Let dry.

Using flat brush, highlight top edges of each holly leaf with green glitter paint. Let dry.

FINISHING: Glue cabochons (acrylic stones) onto sweatshirt, referring to Fig. 1 and photo for placement. Let dry. ❀

HOLLY LEAF PATTERNS

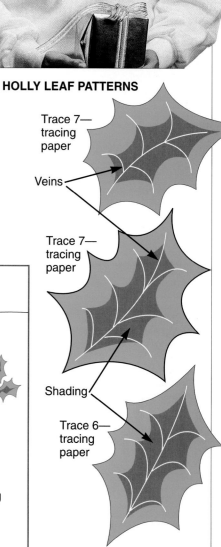

Trace 7—tracing paper

Veins

Trace 7—tracing paper

Shading

Trace 6—tracing paper

HOLLY BERRY PATTERN
Trace 19—tracing paper

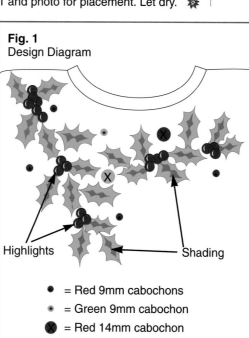

Fig. 1
Design Diagram

Highlights

Shading

● = Red 9mm cabochons
✻ = Green 9mm cabochon
❌ = Red 14mm cabochon
Ⓧ = Green 14mm cabochon

Happy Mouse Covers Gifts in Bright Style

MAKING a home-crafted present even merrier is the task of this happy critter sack you can easily put together. It'll cleverly cover gifts and, later, act as a sweet container for holiday mementos.

Feel free to follow the color scheme that Chris Pfefferkorn of New Braunfels, Texas used for hers, or try combining new tones to make your own.

Materials Needed:
Patterns on this page
Tracing or pattern paper
Pencil
Fabrics—two 7-inch squares of red and white stripe for bag and scrap of green Christmas print for ears
Felt—scraps of gray and white
10 inches of red 1/4-inch-wide rickrack
Satin ribbon—6 inches of 1/4-inch-wide red and 24 inches of 3/8-inch-wide green
Black embroidery thread
Red all-purpose sewing thread
Size 24 embroidery needle
Standard sewing supplies
Fine-line red permanent marker (optional)
Fabric glue
Medium size safety pin
Scissors

Finished Size: Gift bag is 6-1/2 inches wide x 6 inches high. Total design area is 11-3/4 inches wide x 8 inches high.

Directions:
Trace patterns onto tracing paper and cut out. Cut fabrics as indicated on patterns and cut one 2-in. x 2-3/4-in. gift tag from white felt.

ASSEMBLY: Center face on right side of red and white striped fabric, about 1-1/2 in. below top edge, and glue.

Place each hand 1/2 in. below bottom of face as shown in photo. Machine-stitch in place along straight edge, using red thread and wide satin zigzag stitch. Bring threads to back side of fabric and secure.

Pin each inner ear to gray felt outer ear where indicated on pattern. Machine-stitch onto outer ear using red thread and wide satin zigzag stitch.

Write name on gift tag with pencil. Machine-stitch over pencil line with red thread and wide satin zigzag stitch. Or write name on tag with red marker. Machine-stitch rickrack around outside edge of gift tag using red thread. Bring threads to back and secure. Glue gift tag to hands as shown in photo.

Using three strands of black embroidery floss, stitch French knots for eyes and nose as shown in Fig. 1. Using one strand, make three long straight stitches from each side of nose to just beyond the edge of face for whiskers as shown on pattern.

Tie red ribbon into bow and hand-stitch to bottom edge of face. Trim ends at an angle.

With right sides together, pin straight edge of ear to outside edge of bag front, 1 in. from top edge. Repeat with other ear on other side. Pin straight edge of tail 1/2 in. from bottom of right edge of bag, with tail toward center. Pin feet to bottom of bag, 3/4 in. from center with feet pointing away from each other. All pieces will point toward center of right side of bag. Baste in place.

Pin gift bag back to front, right sides together with raw edges matching. Starting 3/4 in. from right front top edge, machine-stitch a 1/4-in. seam, using straight stitch around sides and bottom. Be sure to catch edges of ears, feet and tail in seam and backstitch at beginning and end of seam. Clip threads. Turn bag right side out.

Fold 1/4 in. along top edge to inside of bag. Fold 1/2 in. to inside again and press. Machine-stitch, using straight stitch through all layers close to edge of first fold to form channel for ribbon.

Use safety pin to thread green ribbon through channel at top of gift bag. Knot ribbon ends and trim at an angle. ❁

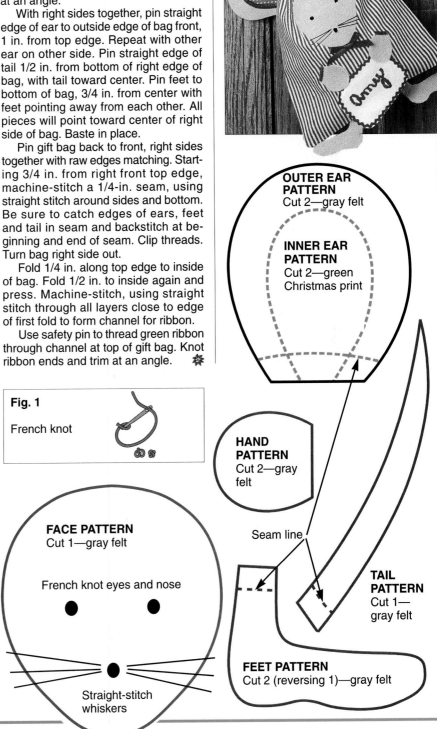

Fig. 1

French knot

OUTER EAR PATTERN
Cut 2—gray felt

INNER EAR PATTERN
Cut 2—green Christmas print

HAND PATTERN
Cut 2—gray felt

TAIL PATTERN
Cut 1—gray felt

Seam line

FACE PATTERN
Cut 1—gray felt

French knot eyes and nose

Straight-stitch whiskers

FEET PATTERN
Cut 2 (reversing 1)—gray felt

Craft Section...

Paper Trims Are Simply Twice as Nice

"PAPERWORK" at this time of year? Karen Taylor's happy holiday type is sure to please!

To make these trims, Karen—who's from Redding, California—turned to two techniques that have paper in common...the art of rolling and shaping paper strips, called quilling, and cross-stitching on perforated paper.

Materials Needed:

Charts on next page
White 14-count perforated paper*—one 4-inch x 4-inch piece for each ornament
DMC six-strand embroidery floss in colors listed on color key
No. 24 or No. 26 tapestry needle
Gold metallic thread for hangers
Tracing paper
8-1/2-inch x 11-inch piece of lightweight cardboard
Corsage pin, round toothpick or quilling tool for rolling paper
Craft knife
1/8-inch-wide quilling paper or construction paper cut into 1/8-inch-wide strips—green and crimson
Straight pin or toothpick
Clear-drying craft glue
Ruler
Pencil

Waxed paper
Scissors

*Perforated paper is available at needlework and craft shops. Or order from the American Needlewoman, P.O. Box 6472, Fort Worth TX 76115; 1-800/433-2231.

Finished Size: The candle ornament is 3 inches across and cross-stitch design is 1-3/8 inches x 1-1/4 inches; house ornament is 4-1/2 inches across and cross-stitch design is 1-3/8 inches square; heart ornament is 3 inches across x 5-1/2 inches long and cross-stitch design is 1 inch square.

Directions:

CROSS-STITCHING: Cut a 4-in. square of perforated paper for each ornament. Measure 2 in. from adjoining edges and mark center of paper lightly with pencil. To find center of chart, draw lines across chart connecting arrows. Begin stitching at this point so design will be centered.

Each square on chart equals one stitch over a set of holes. Separate six-strand embroidery floss and use three strands for all cross-stitches. See Fig. 1.

Do not knot floss on back of work. Instead, leave a short tail of floss on back and hide it under the next few stitches. To end a strand, run needle under a few neighboring stitches before cutting floss.

When stitching is complete, trace patterns for cutting perforated paper onto tracing paper and cut out. Place patterns over cross-stitched areas and trim perforated paper as indicated.

BASIC QUILLING INSTRUCTIONS: To roll paper coils, tear off a strip of 1/8-in.-wide quilling or construction paper to the length specified in the instructions. Moisten one end of the strip slightly and press it onto the center of the corsage pin or toothpick. If using a quilling tool, place paper end in the crevice.

Roll the remaining length of the strip tightly between your thumb and forefinger (without turning the tool), keeping strip's edges even. Slide pin/toothpick/tool out and glue end in place, or allow coil to open to desired size, then glue end in place. Strive for uniformity between like shapes.

When gluing quilled shapes together, use a toothpick to place a drop of glue wherever the shapes touch.

The following shapes are used, as shown in Fig. 2:

Loose Circle: Roll a tight circle without gluing end. Slip it off the tool and let it expand to desired size. Glue the end.

Teardrop: Roll and glue a loose circle. When dry, tightly pinch one side of the circle to a point, allowing the opposite side to stay rounded.

Shaped Teardrop: Make a loose circle and glue end. After gluing, pinch glued end to form a curved point.

Marquise: Roll and glue a loose circle as for teardrop, but pinch circle on opposite sides to points.

Double Scroll: Mark center of strip with a tiny pencil dot. Roll strip from each end toward the center, stopping at the dot.

Open Heart Scroll: Crease strip at center. Gently roll each end of strip in toward crease. Let coils spring out slightly.

V-Scroll: Crease strip at center, then roll toward crease on outside of paper.

FOR ALL ORNAMENTS: Create coils as directed in individual instructions below, noting that lengths given represent lengths of paper strips to tear, not lengths or widths of rolled shapes.

Glue piece of waxed paper to cardboard. Place cross-stitched designs on waxed paper and glue quilled shapes around design as shown on patterns at right, making sure about one-third of quilled shapes are on perforated paper.

After shapes are glued together, allow each ornament to dry, then gently remove from waxed paper.

CANDLE ORNAMENT: Coils/Strips: Use 6-in.-long strips of green paper to make nine double scrolls, eight V-scrolls and two marquise shapes.

Assembly: Referring to Candle pattern at right, position quilled shapes around outside edge of candle cross-stitch. Glue shapes to the perforated paper and to each other wherever they touch.

HOUSE ORNAMENT: Coils/Strips: Use 9-in.-long strips of green paper to make four marquise shapes. Use 6-in.-long strips to make eight loose circles, eight double scrolls and 16 shaped teardrops. Use 12-in.-long strips to make four open heart scrolls.

Assembly: Referring to House pattern at right, position quilled shapes around outside edge of house cross-stitch. Glue into place as for candle ornament.

HEART ORNAMENT: Coils/Strips: Use 12-in.-long strips of crimson paper to make four large shaped teardrops, one large teardrop and one large open heart scroll. Use 6-in.-long strips to

make three small open heart scrolls, two 6-in.-long double scrolls, two V-scrolls (cut one V-scroll in half at center fold), 10 loose circles, six marquise shapes, two small shaped teardrops and one small teardrop.

Assembly: Referring to Heart pattern below, position quilled shapes around outside edge of heart cross-stitch, placing two halves of cut V-scroll on top of the large shaped teardrops at top of trim. Glue into place as for candle ornament.

FINISHING (for all ornaments): Cut a 7-in. length of gold metallic thread and tie it to top of each shape for hanger. ❁

Note: Quilling patterns are actual size.

QUILLED ORNAMENTS COLOR KEY

		DMC
■ Red	. . . .	321
■ Blue	. . . .	322
■ Gold	. . . .	725
■ Green	. . . .	911

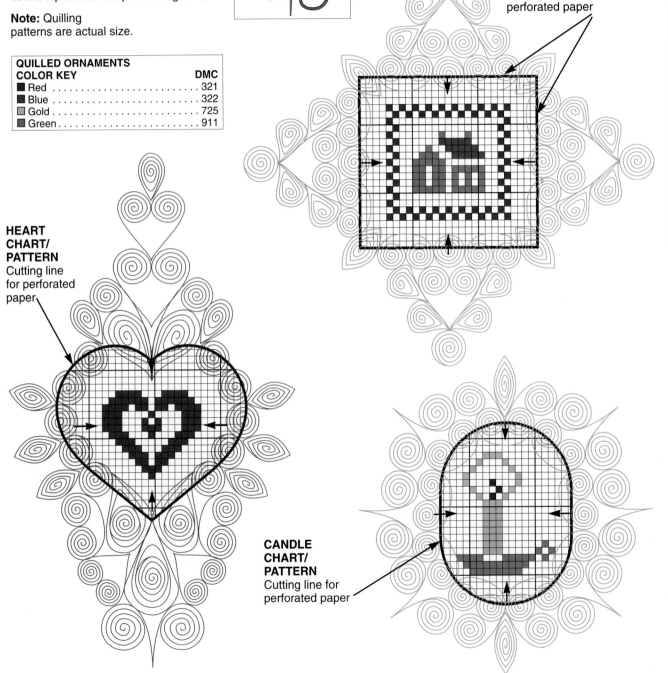

Fig. 2 Quilling shapes

Loose circle
Marquise
Open heart scroll
Teardrop
Double scroll
Shaped teardrop
V-scroll

Fig. 1

HOUSE CHART/PATTERN
Cutting line for perforated paper

HEART CHART/ PATTERN
Cutting line for perforated paper

CANDLE CHART/ PATTERN
Cutting line for perforated paper

Put Lid on Gifts...with Holly-Jolly Toppers

YOU won't be in a jam when it comes to presenting holiday treats, thanks to this oh-sew-special idea from Gayla Cox of Guthrie, Oklahoma.

The process for dressing up pint jars, she reveals, involves cutting out felt covers, then attaching appliqued holly leaf cutouts and pretty ribbons.

Materials Needed (for all three toppers):

Patterns on this page
Tracing or pattern paper
Pencil
Tailor's chalk (optional)
Three 12-ounce canning jars with regular-size metal bands and lids
7-inch squares of felt—two red and one white
Two 6-inch squares of green woven fabric for holly leaves
Scrap of fusible web
One 6-inch-round crocheted doily
Three heart-shaped beads or buttons
Four 8mm red acrylic rhinestones or beads
Three red 1/2-inch pom-poms
All-purpose sewing thread—red and green
No. 24 tapestry needle
48 inches of 3/8-inch-wide green satin ribbon
30 inches of 1/4-inch-wide red satin ribbon
Glue gun and glue sticks or craft glue
Craft knife
Scissors
Standard sewing supplies

Finished Size: Each topper measures 6 inches across and will fit on a regular-size (2-1/2-inch-diameter) canning jar lid.

Directions:
Trace patterns for scalloped circle and holly leaf onto tracing or pattern paper. Cut out.

Place scalloped circle pattern on top of red and white felt squares folded in half. Trace around edges with tailor's chalk or pencil. Cut one white and two red circles to make toppers as shown in photo at left.

Using craft knife or scissors, cut ribbon slits in each circle as shown on pattern.

Following manufacturer's directions, fuse the wrong sides of the green fabric together.

Place the holly leaf pattern on fused fabric and trace around outside edges six times, using tailor's chalk or pencil. Cut out along traced edges for six holly leaves.

Machine-stitch, using wide zigzag satin stitch and matching thread, around all outside edges of each holly leaf. Secure threads and clip.

ASSEMBLY: Red Topper: Glue tips of two holly leaves and three red pom-poms onto center of red scalloped circle as shown in photo.

Thread green ribbon through tapestry needle and weave ribbon through slits in the red circle. Place the topper on top of jar lid and draw ends of ribbon tightly around the lid. Knot the ribbon and tie ends into bow. Trim ends at an angle to desired length.

Secure topper to rim with glue.

White Topper: Glue tips of two holly leaves and glue or sew three red beads or buttons to center of white circle.

Weave red ribbon through slits, tie into a bow and finish topper as directed above.

Red and White Crocheted Topper: Position white crocheted doily on top of red circle, matching outside edges. Place several dots of glue between layers to hold in place.

Glue the tips of two holly leaves and four red beads or rhinestones to the center of crocheted doily.

Weave green ribbon through slits and finish as above. ✿

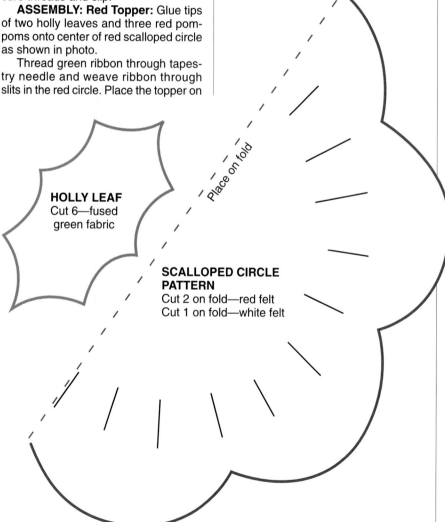

HOLLY LEAF
Cut 6—fused green fabric

Place on fold

SCALLOPED CIRCLE PATTERN
Cut 2 on fold—red felt
Cut 1 on fold—white felt

Trace bell pattern onto the paper side of fusible web three times. Cut around bells on traced lines. Remove paper backing.

Center one bell on hand towel with bottom edge of bell about 4 in. from end of towel. Fuse onto towel, following manufacturer's directions.

Overlap remaining bells as shown in photo at left and center on bath towel about 7 in. from end of towel. Fuse in place.

Using two strands of embroidery floss, blanket-stitch around outside edges of bells on each towel. See Fig. 1.

Tie silver cord or ribbon into a bow and hand-stitch to towel at tops of bells on bath towel. Cut ends of ribbon at an angle. If using cord, knot ends to prevent raveling. ❄

Fig. 1
Blanket stitch

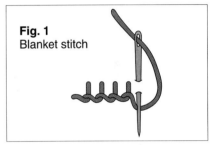

Handy Towels Hit a Happy Holiday Note

RINGING IN the season is good clean fun with these merry terry towels. The bright bells on them chime with appeal!

To make your version of her craft a resounding success, notes Kay Hineman of Rushville, Indiana, be sure to select fabrics and towels in contrasting colors.

Materials Needed (for both towels):
Pattern on this page
Tracing or pattern paper
Pencil
Two terry cloth towels in red or color of choice—one bath-size and one hand-size
Scraps of 100% cotton fabric in contrasting Christmas print
1/8 yard of paper-backed fusible web
White or contrasting color embroidery floss
No. 24 embroidery needle
8 inches of washable silver cord or ribbon
Measuring tape
Scissors
Iron and ironing surface

Finished Size: Each bell is about 4 inches x 4-5/8 inches. Designs will fit on standard-size hand and bath towels.

Directions:
Pre-wash fabrics, including towels, without fabric softeners, washing colors separately. If rinse water is discolored, wash again until water runs clear. Machine-dry and press fabrics.

Trace bell pattern onto tracing or pattern paper. Cut out.

Fuse paper-backed fusible web onto wrong side of Christmas print, following manufacturer's directions.

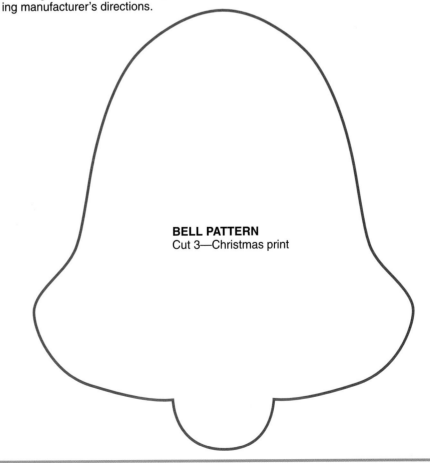

BELL PATTERN
Cut 3—Christmas print

This Tree Grower Gets Around to an Early Christmas

RINGING IN Christmas in a roundabout way is Nancy Richardson's forest forte (top left). Boughs she takes from family trees are rounded up quickly by Midwestern customers "pining" for a homegrown holiday.

THE CUSTOMERS at Nancy Richardson's know best…especially if they've just discovered a hidden gift for garland!

Nancy recalls the day she took leftover pine boughs from her family's Christmas tree farm near Spring Grove, Illinois to piece together a holiday wreath. She spruced it up with pinecones, chestnuts and a bow of country plaid. Then she held it up to get husband George's opinion.

"Lovely!" answered a voice that *wasn't* George's. "I'll take it."

Nancy has been going round and round ever since that unseen customer spoke up. She's the chief wreath decorator in the Richardsons' one-stop evergreen operation. There, you can select and cut your own tree before visiting the barn to pick up a wreath, swag or centerpiece.

Every branch of the family tree's involved in the Yuletide enterprise.

"George and his brother co-own the farmstead—which has been in our family over 150 years—with their parents, Owen and Margaret," reports Nancy. "Our teenage sons, Kyle and Ryan, help drive wagons, shake and bale the trees and carry them to customers' cars. Daughter Emily helps me decorate the wreaths."

Nancy stays close to home as well in assembling ingredients for her wreaths, made mostly from natural materials. "I don't have to stray too far from the farm to find bright berries, pinecones and homegrown oregano," she confirms. "With my centerpieces and swags, I often mix several different types of pine greens together."

As much as the holidays are the hub of the hubbub for the Richardsons, their farming version of Santa's workshop keeps Nancy and her family busy year-round. Trees need to be trimmed and watered in summer, while wreath-making comes around in early November.

When Christmastime itself arrives, the excitement increases. George takes customers out to the woods in a hay wagon, where they can pick from 3,500 Scotch and white pines, Douglas firs and Norway spruces. Afterward, there's hot cider and warm cheer in the wreath barn…and, of course, plenty of Nancy's needle work to admire.

Beams Nancy, "It's the best feeling in the world to work on something, then to hold it up and hear someone say, 'That's just what I wanted!' "

This country wreath maker heard those words from her first customer. They still have her going in circles…and smiling every evergreen inch of the way.

Editor's Note: *The Richardson farm is open from 10 a.m. to dusk starting the day after Thanksgiving. For more information, write to Nancy Richardson, 9407 Richardson Rd., Spring Grove IL 60081 (enclose a self-addressed stamped envelope). Or phone her at 1-815/675-2011.*

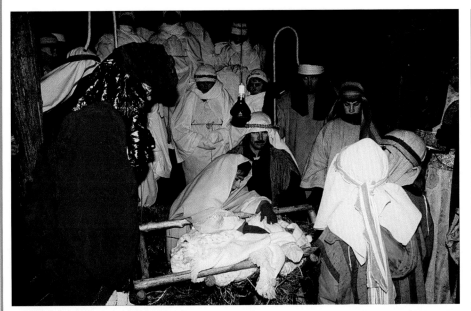

'Mary' Finds a Way in Manger To Make Dream Come True

WHEN she was a young girl playing Mary in the Sunday school Christmas pageant, Linda Hagedorn dreamed of bringing the story to life in a real stable.

Now that she's all grown up, the dream's an inspiring reality she and her family annually share with hundreds of others. This holiday season, the South Dakotans are embarking on the 20th year of presenting *Journey to Bethlehem*.

"When we moved here, I realized we had everything needed to stage a live outdoor pageant," Linda relates from her family's Sioux Falls farm. "There was a barn, a circular drive, parking…even a room where people could warm up after."

Linda's husband, Roger, agreed. And when she suggested the idea at the Evangelical Congregation Church, helping hands were everywhere to be found.

In the spirit of the season, church members volunteered to write the script and record music, sew costumes, prepare the buildings, bake cookies and park cars.

To fill a role, a neighbor donat-

GLORIOUS STORY of Nativity is retold at Linda Hagedorn's family farmstead. Whether outfitting magi or guiding shepherds to barn theater, Linda keeps real Christmas spirit shining.

ed his donkey. A family from the congregation cast its cow in a supporting part.

"The memory of that original Christmas pageant will always stick with me," Linda reminisces. "Perhaps for the first time, people—of all ages—could see Christmas as a 'real' event. The cobwebbed barn gave us all an understanding of what it might have been like on the first Christmas."

Journey to Bethlehem, held the weekend before Christmas each year, begins with music and a reading of the Christmas story. Mary and Joseph arrive at the inn by donkey and are told there's no room. After they're shown to the barn, shepherds and wise men arrive, and the innkeeper invites the crowd to see the newborn Baby Jesus.

Filling that starring role occasionally causes last-minute panic. "Once, the baby didn't arrive in time," Linda explains, remembering a frantic trip to the mall in search of a life-like doll.

"Then I spotted a couple with a baby and asked if they'd like their newborn to play a very important part. They were hesitant at first—but later they were thrilled."

Over the past two decades, thousands of people have flocked to the farm for the performances—with some 1,200 people squeezing in during one. "It was so crowded," Linda laughs, "that the innkeeper couldn't move from the barn window to beckon the people in to see the baby!"

Seeing the "real" Baby Jesus never fails to move onlookers, no matter their age. "One year, a 3-year-old boy made his way through the crowd and all the way up to the manger," Linda reverently recalls. "He pulled a little teddy bear out of his pocket and laid it on the straw next to the baby. It was his gift to the Christ Child."

With memories like those as payment, Linda and her crew plan to keep giving *their* gift to the community for years to come.

Editor's Note: *For dates and times of the Journey to Bethlehem performances, write to Linda Hagedorn, 46954-272nd St., Tea SD 57064 (enclose a self-addressed stamped envelope). Or phone her at 1-605/368-2930.* ❈

The Perfect Tree

A fiction story by Roxana Chalmers of Sedalia, Colorado

PINPOINTS of blue beams and a host of lacy white angels filled Rebecca's eyes. No question, she concluded…*this* was the prettiest Christmas tree she'd ever seen!

Rebecca had managed to steal away to town to do a little gift shopping—and a little dreaming. The tree she'd spotted here in the store—its lights sparkling like jewels and garland glittering like gold—was just the type she longed to have in her own home. But that, she knew, wasn't possible.

No, she chuckled silently, *not at all possible!* She didn't dare decorate the Christmas tree without 6-year-old Katy and 4-year-old twins Kevin and Jody participating. And their "help" guaranteed a tree festooned with construction-paper chains and drooping under the burden of homemade clay Santas…

A few days later, Rebecca, husband Tom and the children tromped around their forested land, trying to decide which tree was the "perfect" one this year. With so many candidates, choosing wasn't easy.

Then little Katy piped up. "Why," she wondered, "do we have to pick just one? They're all so pretty!"

Rebecca opened her mouth to explain—then suddenly stopped. *Why indeed?* she asked herself. *Why can't there be a tree in the den for the children to decorate…and another one in the living room for me?*

Not long after, the children's tree was set up in the den. While Tom strung the lights, Katy, Kevin and Jody came up with decorations. Mixing with old favorites from the ornament box were small trucks, dolls and plastic warriors. Three teddy bears, dangling from the tree by shoelaces, weighted their branches down to the floor.

"It's the most best tree that we've ever

had," little Jody declared proudly.

"When are we going to do the other tree?" Katy inquired.

"Oh, I'll work on it tomorrow," Rebecca answered.

Kevin's forehead scrunched up. "All by yourself?"

Tom winked at Rebecca. "I think your mother wants to give something a try," he said.

The next morning, Rebecca took inventory of the ornaments. The children had used all the reds and greens, leaving mostly blue lights and silver balls. Blue and silver would be just lovely, she resolved. But she'd need more than balls and pretty lights.

Rebecca rummaged through her boxes of ribbons and lace and found a roll of silvery gauze she'd bought at an after-Christmas sale the year before. Just perfect for big soft bows, she mused to herself.

Her boxes yielded enough material for 20 bows tied with rosettes of blue ribbon. They gave the tree an elegant Victorian look.

Rebecca stood back to admire her handiwork. It *was* lovely. Somehow, though, something didn't seem right.

Tom had taken the children along to feed the cattle. Just as Rebecca was adding a few finishing touches, they returned, hungry for lunch.

"Didn't you have any other color lights except blue?" asked Kevin. "You can borrow some of ours."

"These ribbons are pretty," Katy said, fingering the bows. "Can we have some for our tree?"

Rebecca hesitated, envisioning the bare spots that would be left on her tree.

"We could trade," Katy pressed.

Katy's earnest expression made the decision easy—Rebecca traded three bows with Katy for three items from the children's tree. Then she made a similar exchange with each of the boys.

That afternoon, Katy called Rebecca into the living room from the kitchen. The tree, minus nine of its blue and silver bows, sported two red balls, three miniature dolls with tinsel halos, two plastic cars and two teddy bears.

Rebecca crossed her arms and studied the tree carefully. *Not exactly a showroom tree anymore*, she determined, a smile flitting across her face.

"Come here, you guys," she chirped, opening her arms wide for a triple hug. "You had the right idea. Now, my tree looks like a *Christmas* tree!"

North Pole's Just the Start For the Santas She Sculpts

IN the talented hands of ex-art teacher Darlene Bushmaker, Santa rates as world Claus.

"Before I started designing my own Santa dolls," she reports from her at-home workshop in Mosinee, Wisconsin, "I took some time to investigate his origins. I quickly learned what he wore depended on where he was."

Which is why her Clauses aren't always the ones your eyes might be most accustomed to.

The Belsnickel Santa of Germany, for instance, is outfitted in a cloak of fur and leather to keep him warm through the long and harsh winters of northern Europe. English Father Christmas wears a woolen white cape and a crown of holly.

A more familiar fellow is the North American Voyager Darlene designed. The Santa from this side of the sea sports a furry cap and fringed coat, and he bears presents sure to delight all the pioneer children on his list—wooden skis, a birdhouse of birch bark and a red-flannel teddy bear.

"To make my Santas, I use wire, dowels and plaster for the body, and modeling material for the hands and face," she explains. "My husband,

Keith, gets into the act by cutting the wooden bases for the Santas to stand on.

"I sew all the clothing myself, down to the shoes, belts and mittens. For material, I scour antique shops, flea markets and garage sales for vintage wool, linen, lace and furs. In addition, I make sure that, among all the treats and toys, each of my Santas carries an American flag."

Her heritage figures in another way in what she does. With every Santa she "dolls up", Darlene notes, she remembers the eagerly anticipated Christmases she enjoyed while she was growing up in rural Minnesota.

"The whole town would turn out for our Christmas program," she recalls. "The most exciting part to me was at the end, when our families would start singing, 'Here comes Santa Claus…' With that, the jolly old elf himself would burst into the room and hand each of us a big bag of peanuts, oranges and hard candy.

"Afterward, I'd wonder just who Santa was and where he came from. That's exactly the mystery and excitement of childhood I hope *my* Santas inspire today."

Editor's Note: *For information on Darlene's Santas, contact her at Du Bay Arts, 2272 Du Bay Dr., Mosinee WI 54455; 1-715/457-2588.* ❄

SANTA FAN Darlene Bushmaker (at top) fashions nostalgic Nicks filled with Christmas fun. Her Clauses call numerous nations home.

Sharp, Snugly Ornaments Have You Knitting Pretty

YOU'LL GLIDE through the season in style with these knitted trims.

Christine Ballentine of Attica, Michigan designed the mini mittens and snazzy skates to beautify boughs or top off a special gift. But there's more to them than that. With a little imagination, you can also easily make them into pins!

Materials Needed (for mittens):
Small amounts of worsted-weight yarn—green (with silver thread), white and red
Size 6 (4mm) straight knitting needles
Tapestry needle
Size D/3 (3.25mm) crochet hook
2-1/3 yards of 1/8-inch-wide red satin ribbon
Tacky (white) glue
Scissors

Gauge: In St st, 4 sts and 6 rows = 1 inch.

Stitch Used:
STOCKINETTE STITCH: St st
   Row 1: Knit.
   Row 2: Purl.
   Repeat Rows 1 and 2.

Directions:
MITTENS (make two): Cuff: With white, cast on 17 sts, leaving an 8-in. end.
   Rows 1-6: K 1, p 1 across to last st, k 1. Fasten off white.
   Row 7: Attaching green, k 7, k 2 tog, k 8: 16 sts.
   Row 8: Purl.
   Row 9: K 7, inc in each of next 2 sts, k 7: 18 sts.
   Row 10: Purl.
   Row 11: K 7, inc in next st, k 2, inc in next st, k 7: 20 sts.
   Row 12: Purl.
   Row 13: K 7, inc in next st, k 4, inc in next st, k 7: 22 sts.
   Row 14: Purl.
   Row 15: K 7, inc in next st, k 6, inc in next st, k 7: 24 sts.
   Row 16: P 16, turn.
   Thumb: K 8, turn, p 8, turn, (k 2 tog) four times: 4 thumb sts remain. Break yarn. With tapestry needle, draw yarn through thumb sts left on needle.
   With purl side facing, attach green at thumb, p 8 (remaining sts of Row 16).

   Rows 17-22: Work in St st across remaining 16 sts.
   Row 23: K 2 tog across: 8 sts.
   Break yarn and draw through 8 sts left on needle. Weave in any loose ends.
   Use matching yarn to sew thumb and side seams.
   Finishing: With red yarn, crochet a 10-in. chain. Attach an end to upper edge of each mitten. Tie bow in center of chain.
   Using three 7-in. pieces of satin ribbon held together for each side, make four bows and glue in place on the mittens, centered just below the cuff.

Materials Needed (for ice skates):
Small amounts of worsted-weight yarn—black, red and white
Four 1/4-inch green pom-poms
Two jumbo paper clips, each 1-7/8 inches long
Small amount of polyester stuffing
Size 5 (3.75mm) or 6 (4mm) straight knitting needles
Size D/3 (3.25mm) crochet hook
Tapestry needle
Tacky (white) glue
Scissors

Stitch Used: See Stitch Used for the mittens at left.

Directions:
SKATES (make two): Beginning at bottom with black, cast on 18 sts, leaving an 8-in. strand of yarn.
   Row 1: Purl. Fasten off black.
   Row 2 (RS): Attaching white, knit.
   Rows 3, 5, 7 and 9: Purl.
   Row 4: K 1, k 2 tog, k 4, k 2 tog two times, k 4, k 2 tog, k 1: 14 sts.
   Row 6: K 1, k 2 tog, k 8, k 2 tog, k 1: 12 sts.
   Row 8: K 1, k 2 tog, k 6, k 2 tog, k 1: 10 sts.
   Rows 10-13: Work in St st.
   Rows 14-16: Purl.
   Bind off loosely. Break yarn, leaving about an 8-in. strand. Fold skate in half, right side out, matching ends of rows. Using matching yarns, sew sole and front seam. Stuff firmly and sew top seam closed. Repeat for second skate.
   Add red yarn laces as shown in photo, tying ends in bow at top of each skate.
   Finishing: With red yarn, crochet a 10-in. chain. Attach one end to top back of each skate. Tie bow in center of chain.
   Hook paper clip through knit stitches at bottom of skate. Add dots of glue to secure paper clip to bottom. Glue pompoms to ends of laces. Let dry. ❄

ABBREVIATIONS	
inc	increase
k	knit
p	purl
RS	right side
st(s)	stitch(es)
St st	Stockinette stitch
tog	together

Frame Picture-Perfect Stitches

CATCH A GLIMPSE of a country Christmas in these sampler scenes crafted by Barbara Hicks Robinson of Wellington, Nevada.

The frame is really a little hoop that keeps cloth taut as you're stitching. Later, it adds a festive flourish to your Christmas tree.

Materials Needed (for both ornaments):

Charts on this page
Two 5-inch x 6-inch pieces of white 14-count Aida cloth
DMC six-strand embroidery floss in colors listed on color key
Size 24 tapestry needle
Two 3-inch x 4-inch oval red hoops (Barbara used Flexi-Hoops, one with screw clamp along long edge and one with screw clamp along short edge)
Two 12-inch pieces of 1/4-inch-wide green satin ribbon
Two 4-inch x 3-1/4-inch pieces of white craft felt
Pencil
Tacky (white) glue
Scissors
Heavy book (for weight)

Finished Size: Each ornament is 3-3/4 inches x 3 inches. The design area of the Peace ornament is 41 stitches wide x 32 stitches high and the design area of the Noel ornament is 29 stitches wide x 38 stitches high.

Directions:

STITCHING: Zigzag or overcast the edges of the fabric to prevent fraying. Fold cloth in half lengthwise, then fold in half crosswise to determine center and mark this point. To find the center of each chart, draw lines across chart connecting arrows. Begin stitching at this point so design will be centered.

Separate six-strand floss and use three strands for all cross-stitching and two strands for all backstitching. See stitch illustrations in Fig. 1 below right.

Each square on chart equals one stitch over a set of fabric threads. Use colors on color key to complete cross-stitching, then backstitching.

Do not knot floss on back of work. Instead, leave a short tail on back of work and hold in place. Weave tails and ends through several stitches as stitching progresses.

When all stitching is completed, and only if necessary, wash the stitched piece gently in lukewarm water and press right side down on terry towel to dry.

FRAMING: Insert stitched piece in hoop, centering design. Turn hoop over to wrong side and trim the stitched piece as close as possible to the edges of the hoop.

Place hoop on top of felt and trace around edge. Draw another line 1/8 in. inside of traced line and cut on this line. Glue felt oval onto back of hoop, covering raw edges of stitched piece. Weight down with heavy book until dry.

Tie ribbon in a bow around screw clamp of hoop. Trim ribbon ends diagonally. ❀

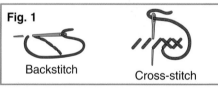

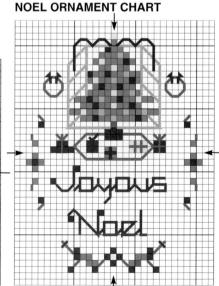

Fig. 1

Backstitch   Cross-stitch

COLOR KEY — DMC

- ⊡ White
- ▨ Light Brown . . 436
- ▨ Red 666
- ▨ Dark Green . . 700
- ☐ Light Gold . . . 725
- ▨ Light Blue . . . 828
- ▨ Light Green . . 954
- ▨ Bright Blue . . . 996

BACKSTITCHING

- — Dark Green . . 700
- — Red 666
- — Medium Gold . 729

PEACE ORNAMENT CHART

NOEL ORNAMENT CHART

Album Preserves Precious Memories

CHRISTMAS KEEPSAKES can all come together in one convenient place when you assemble this beautified binder to store memories of the season.

Irma Fredrickson of Stewartville, Minnesota designed the quilted album after rediscovering a letter she'd written to Santa when she was a little girl.

"My children's special cards and pageant programs as well as letters from friends are included in it," she details. "Now, I'm beginning to add my grandchildren's drawings, too!"

Materials Needed:
Patterns on page 98
One 1-1/2-inch ring binder
1 yard of 44-inch-wide 100% cotton white-and-red print fabric for outside cover and inside flaps
1/4 yard or scraps of the following 100% cotton fabrics—red, green and white Christmas prints for gifts; white Christmas print for tree; green solid for tree, tree trunk and base;

light, medium and dark gold solids or tiny prints for star beams, star and halo; ivory solid for face; blue check for blanket; gray solid for manger
13-inch x 25-inch piece of muslin for lining
13-inch x 25-inch piece of lightweight batting
2-1/4 yards of red purchased piping
Buttons—eight red 7/16-inch round, six green 5/8-inch round, two white small bow-shaped and two red large bow-shaped novelty buttons
Thread to match fabrics
Hand-sewing needle
Standard sewing supplies
Scissors
Rotary cutter and mat (optional)
Quilter's ruler (optional)
Tracing paper and pencil
Water-soluble marker
Iron and ironing surface
Masking tape (optional)

Finished Size: Cover is 24 inches wide x 12 inches high.

Directions:
Machine-wash, dry and press all fabrics. Use a scant 1/4-in. seam allowance for all machine stitching. Turn fabric under a scant 1/4 in. on all raw edges when hand-appliqueing.

Trace pattern pieces on page 98 onto tracing paper with pencil. (To complete star beam patterns, trace both sections of each star beam separately, then join the two pieces for each beam by matching the letters at the ends of the pattern lines—joining A to A, B to B, C to C, etc.)

Place each applique pattern on right side of fabric as directed and trace around it with a water-soluble marker. Cut out patterns.

CUTTING: From white-and-red print, cut one 13-in. x 25-in. piece for outside cover, two 13-in. x 12-in. pieces for inside flaps and two 1-in. x 4-1/2-in. pieces for inside facings.

From green solid, cut one 2-in. x 44-in. strip and one 5-3/8-in. square for tree. For tree trunk, cut one 1-1/2-in. x 2-in. rectangle. From the 2-in. strip, cut ten 2-in. squares, then cut each square in half diagonally for 20 small triangles. Cut the 5-3/8-in. square in half diagonally for two large triangles, setting one triangle aside for another project.

From white Christmas print, cut one 2-in. x 44-in. strip, one 1-5/8-in. square for tree and one 1-1/2-in. square for small gift. From the 2-in. strip, cut nine 2-in. squares, then cut each square in half diagonally for 18 small triangles, setting aside one small triangle for another project.

From red Christmas print, cut one 1-5/8-in. x 2-in. rectangle and one 2-in. x 2-1/2-in. rectangle for two gift boxes. From green Christmas print, cut one 2-1/4-in. square for one gift box.

TREE: With right sides together, machine-stitch 17 white Christmas print triangles to 17 matching green solid triangles, stitching along the diagonal cut edge to form 17 half-triangle squares. See Fig. 1.

Press seams toward the darker fabric whenever possible. Trim the triangle points even with pieced edges when necessary.

Row 1: Stitch four half-triangle squares together, following Fig. 2 for color placement.

Row 2: Stitch four half-triangle squares and the 1-5/8-in. white square together, following Fig. 3.

Row 3: Stitch four half-triangle

squares and one small green solid triangle together, following Fig. 4.

Row 4: Paying careful attention to the position of the colors, stitch five half-triangle squares and one small green solid triangle together, following Fig. 5.

TREE ASSEMBLY: Stitch Row 1 to the large green solid triangle, following Fig. 6. Then add Row 2 as shown in Fig. 6. Press both seams toward the large green solid triangle.

Place Row 3, right sides together, along top of Row 1 and end of Row 2, following Fig. 7. Pin carefully so corners of blocks match exactly. Machine-stitch together. Press seam toward Row 3.

Place Row 4, right sides together, along top of Row 2 and end of Row 3, following Fig. 7. Pin carefully so corners of blocks match exactly. Machine-stitch together. Press seam toward Row 4.

STAR BEAMS: Machine-stitch light gold star beam to the medium gold beam and press seam toward the medium gold beam.

Machine-stitch dark gold beam to medium gold beam and press seam toward dark gold beam.

STAR: Referring to Fig. 8, pin three medium gold triangles to every other straight edge of dark gold star center to form triangular star center. Machine-stitch the pieces together.

Pin light gold outside points to sides of each of the three remaining medium gold triangles as shown in Fig. 9, creat-ing three outside point-triangle sets. Machine-stitch each set together.

Pin straight edges of outside point-triangle sets to sides of star center to form star, following Fig. 10. Machine-stitch pieces together.

ASSEMBLY: Following Assembly/Quilting Diagram on page 98, pin tree trunk, green solid triangle tree base, tree, star and star beams to outside cover.

Arrange the Nativity pieces in the following order: halo, face, blanket, manger and manger legs. Pin pieces into place on outside cover.

Hand-applique pieces, turning under only those edges not covered by other overlapping pieces.

Press under raw edges of the gift box pieces and position under the tree as shown in the Assembly/Quilting Diagram. Pin pieces to secure. Hand-applique to the outside cover.

QUILTING: Place muslin on flat surface, taking care to smooth out all wrinkles. Place batting on top of muslin. Place appliqued outside cover on top of batting, right side up, again smoothing out any wrinkles.

Hand-baste or pin all layers together, starting in the center and working diagonally toward outside edges.

Hand-quilt tree following Assembly/Quilting diagram on page 98. Use masking tape, if desired, as a guide to help stitch straight lines. (Be sure to remove tape promptly to avoid getting tape residue on fabrics.) Hand-quilt around inside and outside edge of star, around edges of beams, halo, face, blanket and crib. Remove pins or basting stitches.

FINISHING: Hand-stitch buttons randomly onto tree and bow buttons onto gift boxes. Open binder, lay it flat and center front cover of binder over tree on appliqued cover. Trace around outside edges of binder with water-soluble marker. Remove binder.

Position the red piping around traced line with raw edges facing out and the finished edge of piping facing toward the center. Pin piping in place, overlapping ends. Hand-baste or machine-baste the piping in place. Trim seam to 1/2 in. Set aside.

Machine-stitch a 1-in. hem on one 13-in. edge of each of the inside flaps. Place inside flaps on right and left sides of applique cover with right sides together. Pin in place.

Pin inside facings over piping not covered by flaps, overlapping flaps by 1/2 in. With piping side up, machine-stitch just inside basting stitch (to conceal previous seam) through all layers. Trim seam to 1/4 in.

Turn piece right side out. Hand-stitch facing to muslin backing, turning raw edge under as you stitch.

Fold the binder covers back and insert the binder into the flaps on the inside of the appliqued cover.

(Patterns are on the next page)

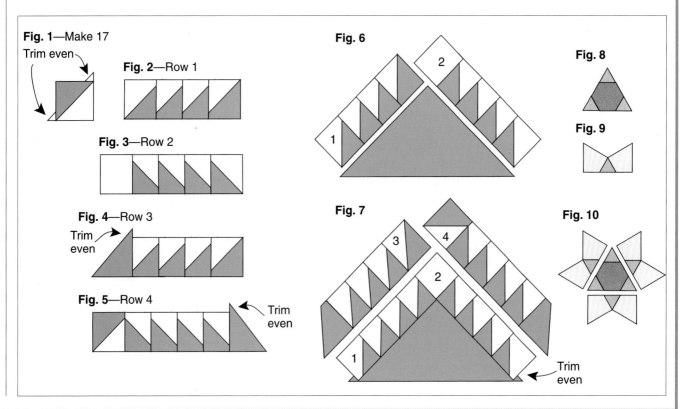

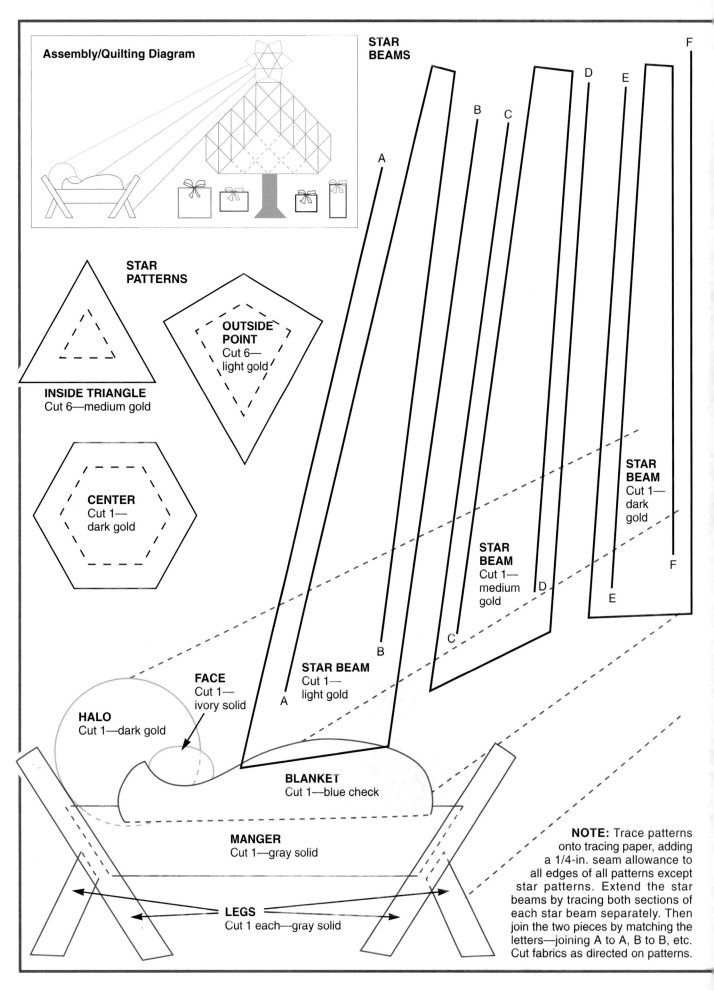

Assembly/Quilting Diagram

STAR BEAMS

F
E
D
C
B
A

STAR PATTERNS

OUTSIDE POINT
Cut 6—
light gold

INSIDE TRIANGLE
Cut 6—medium gold

CENTER
Cut 1—
dark gold

STAR BEAM
Cut 1—
dark gold

F

E

STAR BEAM
Cut 1—
medium gold

D

C

B

STAR BEAM
Cut 1—
light gold

A

FACE
Cut 1—
ivory solid

HALO
Cut 1—dark gold

BLANKET
Cut 1—blue check

MANGER
Cut 1—gray solid

LEGS
Cut 1 each—gray solid

NOTE: Trace patterns onto tracing paper, adding a 1/4-in. seam allowance to all edges of all patterns except star patterns. Extend the star beams by tracing both sections of each star beam separately. Then join the two pieces by matching the letters—joining A to A, B to B, etc. Cut fabrics as directed on patterns.

Manger Keeps Holiday Meaning

THE MIRACLE of Christmas comes alive in a child's hands with this modeling clay creche. Mary and Joseph can be used for decoration or as finger puppets, shares country crafter Karen Taylor of Redding, California.

Materials Needed:
Patterns on this page
Tracing paper
Pencil
Oven-bake polymer clay—flesh, light blue pearl, lavender, green, brilliant blue, brown, bronze and white*
Waxed paper
Craft knife
Rolling pin
Brown paper grocery sack
Transparent tape
Scissors
Toothpicks
Four black seed beads for eyes
E-6000 adhesive or Craftsman's Goop
Polymer clay glaze and paintbrush (optional)
*Karen used Sculpey III clay and Sculpey glaze.

Finished Size: Mary and Joseph are approximately 3-1/2 inches tall. The manger is 1-1/2 inches x 1-1/4 inches. Baby Jesus is 1-1/4 inches long.

Directions:
Begin with clean hands, washing each time you use a new color. Knead pieces of polymer clay until soft and smooth.

Roll out clay between sheets of waxed paper. Lay clay, still on waxed paper, on a cutting board or piece of cardboard when cutting out pieces. When joining pieces, work together with a knife or press into place firmly to avoid having them come apart during baking.

After shaping, bake clay pieces according to manufacturer's directions. Avoid overbaking and allow to cool.

Trace patterns onto tracing paper and cut out.

SHAPING DIRECTIONS: Mary and Joseph: Trace around paper cone onto grocery sack twice, cut out and form into two pointed cones. Tape overlapping edge to hold in place.

For Mary's robe, roll out lavender clay to 1/8-in. thickness and wrap around paper cone. Using a craft knife, trim as necessary at bottom of cone and at seam where edges of clay meet. Remove any excess clay at top of cone. Smooth with fingers.

Repeat with green for Joseph's robe.

Roll a 3/16-in.-thick cylinder of light blue pearl, making it about 5 in. long. Wrap around bottom of cone for trim on Mary's robe. Smooth joining. Repeat for Joseph's robe, using brilliant blue.

From flesh, make two 7/8-in. balls. Press one down over each cone point to form heads for Mary and Joseph.

Roll out light blue pearl to 1/8-in. thickness and cut yoke, using pattern. Press in place on front of Mary's robe.

From lavender, make two 1/2-in. balls and shape into Mary's arms. Press firmly onto each side of body, using a toothpick and fingers to flatten and blend into body under head. Roll two small balls of flesh and press onto robe at end of each arm for hands. From brown, roll several very thin cylinders for hair. (The entire head does not need to be covered with hair, as cloak covers most of head.)

Make Joseph's arms from green and hands from flesh as directed above. Roll very thin cylinders of brown for hair, beard and mustache. Place on Joseph's head as directed above and on his face as shown in photo above right.

Press beads into faces for eyes on Mary and Joseph as shown in photo.

Roll out light blue pearl to 1/8-in. thickness. Cut out cloak according to cloak pattern. Place one edge of light blue pearl cloak on top of Mary's head. Press in place at top of head, along sides of head and along robe. Flare edges slightly at bottom. Repeat with brilliant blue for Joseph.

Roll two 3/16-in.-thick bronze cylinders about 3-1/2 in. long. Form into circle and smooth joining. Press a circle on top of Mary's and Joseph's heads.

Manger: Roll out brown to 1/8-in. thickness and cut manger pieces, following patterns. Form body of manger by pressing side and end pieces together, referring to pattern for joining. Leave leg pieces separate for baking. Lay manger on one side when baking.

Baby Jesus: Make a small 3/8-in. teardrop from flesh for head. Roll a very small cylinder from bronze and form it into circle for halo. Place halo at top of teardrop. Roll out a piece of white to 1/8-in. thickness and cut swaddling cloth according to pattern. Wrap cloth around base of head and fold as shown in photo. After making sure baby will fit into manger, press pieces together to hold.

FINISHING: Bake as directed and allow to cool. Remove paper cones. Glue manger together. If desired, brush glaze onto pieces and allow to dry. ❁

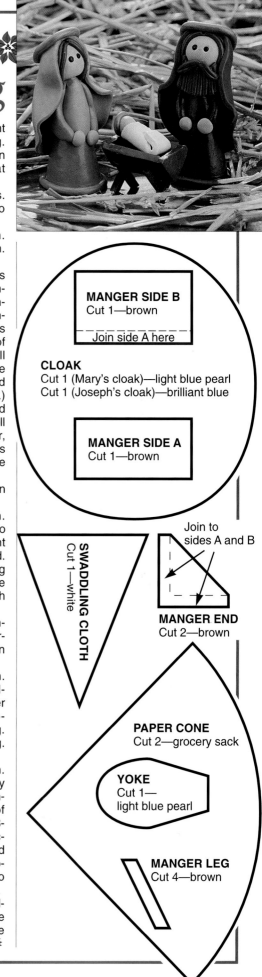

MANGER SIDE B
Cut 1—brown

Join side A here

CLOAK
Cut 1 (Mary's cloak)—light blue pearl
Cut 1 (Joseph's cloak)—brilliant blue

MANGER SIDE A
Cut 1—brown

SWADDLING CLOTH
Cut 1—white

Join to sides A and B

MANGER END
Cut 2—brown

PAPER CONE
Cut 2—grocery sack

YOKE
Cut 1—light blue pearl

MANGER LEG
Cut 4—brown

Wooden Angels Ring Out with Joy

HARK! These herald angels bring glad tidings whether they alight on the fireplace mantel or among other decorations. No matter where they stand, they're always in perfect harmony.

Nancy Chadwell reveals crafters have an array of choices with the angels. "You can stain instead of painting them or add hair and faces," she pens from her Clinton Corners, New York home.

Materials Needed:
Pattern at right
Tracing paper
Pencil
Three 4-inch squares of 1-inch pine
Scroll or coping saw
Sandpaper
Tack cloth
Holly leaf and alphabet stencils*
White and pink acrylic craft paints
Red and green stencil paint
Paintbrushes—1-inch flat and fine-liner
Stencil brush or sponge (optional)
Paper plate or palette
Tacky (white) glue
Fifteen 6mm gold jingle bells
12 inches of 1/8-inch-wide red satin ribbon
Drill with 3/32-inch bit
Scissors
Toothpick
Masking tape
*Nancy used purchased holly and alphabet stencils. You can do the same or paint each onto angels freehand.

Finished Size: Each angel measures about 4 inches high x 4 inches wide.

Directions:
Trace angel pattern below onto tracing paper and cut out.

Trace around angel with pencil on each 4-in. square of wood. Cut out each angel with a scroll or coping saw.

Drill five holes 1/4 in. apart and 1/8 in. deep across top of each head, centered between front and back edges.

Sand wood pieces smooth and wipe with tack cloth to remove sanding dust.

PAINTING: With flat brush, paint each body white and each head pink. Apply a second coat of paint as needed for complete coverage. Let dry between coats.

Tape holly stencil to bottom edge of one angel as shown on pattern. With green and an almost-dry stencil brush or sponge, stencil holly leaves, using an up-and-down motion. Remove stencil and repeat for two remaining angels. Or paint holly freehand, using green and liner brush and following painting illustration (Fig. 1 on page 101, below right).

Dip handle of fine-liner in red paint and dab tiny dots for holly berries, referring to photo at left and Fig.1 for placement.

Stencil red letters onto each angel, following stenciling directions above. Or paint "J", "O" and "Y" on freehand following Fig. 1.

Use toothpick to place hangers of bells into drilled holes on tops of angels' heads and glue into place.

Cut ribbon into three 4-in. pieces and tie each piece into a 1-in. bow. Glue bows onto fronts below heads. ❀

ANGEL PATTERN Cut 3—1-in. pine

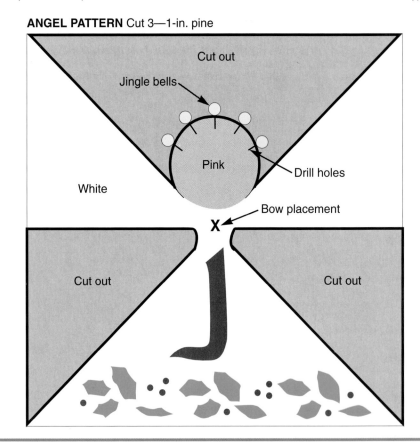

Noel Surrounds Painted Necklace—in No Time!

HANGING *these* stockings with care will warm up your wardrobe in a brand-new fashion. What's more, the necklace is a shoo-in as a top gift idea, too.

The project—from Verlyn King of Tremonton, Utah—is a swift one. All you have to do is paint colorful designs on the stocking cutouts, then string them up with a bunch of beads.

Materials Needed:

Three purchased birch plywood or balsa wood stockings, each 1-3/4 inches tall x 1/8 inch thick*
Sandpaper
Tack cloth
Tracing paper, transfer paper and a stylus or a dry ballpoint pen (optional)
Pencil
Drill and 3/32-inch bit
Acrylic craft paints—white, red, green, medium blue and yellow
Acrylic sealer
Paintbrushes—1/4-inch flat and fine-liner
Paper plate or palette
Black permanent fine-line marker
1/8-inch-wide satin ribbon—28 inches of white, 3 inches of red, 3 inches of green and 3 inches of light blue
Pony beads—four white, two red, two green and two blue
Scissors
No. 26 tapestry needle
Tacky (white) glue

*The stockings are available at most craft stores or from Plum Fun Wood Products, 5427 S.E. 72nd Ave., Portland OR 97206; 1-800/336-6688.

Finished Size: Necklace is 14 inches long. Stockings are 1-3/4 inches tall.

Directions:
Drill holes in wood stockings as indicated on painting patterns. Sand stockings smooth and wipe with tack cloth to remove sanding dust.

Trace painting patterns onto tracing paper and transfer onto stockings with transfer paper and stylus or dry ballpoint pen, or paint designs on freehand.

PAINTING: Place small amounts of each color paint on paper plate or palette as needed.

Patterns and designs are painted on both sides of the wood stockings. Apply a second coat if needed for complete coverage and let all paints dry thoroughly between applications.

With flat brush, paint stockings white. Apply a second coat if needed.

Following painting patterns and using flat brush, paint toes and heels of each stocking, using colors indicated on painting patterns and photo at right.

With fine-liner, paint patterns on stockings as shown.

Paint polka dots by dipping handle of brush into paint and adding dots in a random pattern.

Use marker to paint stitching lines as shown on pattern.

Apply sealer with flat brush.

FINISHING: String pony beads onto white ribbon in the following order: One white, two blue, one white, two red, one white and two green. Tie ribbon together about 1 in. from ends.

Using needle, thread 3-in.-long ribbons through drilled holes of stockings and tie onto white ribbon as in photo.

Apply a dot of glue to each knot to secure. To prevent raveling, cut ends of ribbons at an angle to desired length. ❉

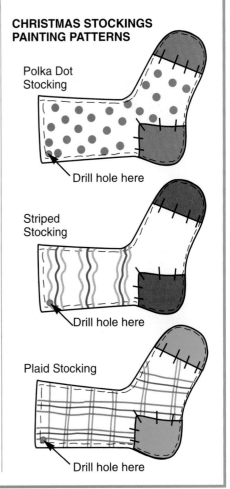

CHRISTMAS STOCKINGS PAINTING PATTERNS

Polka Dot Stocking

Drill hole here

Striped Stocking

Drill hole here

Plaid Stocking

Drill hole here

Fig. 1
Painting Illustration

thread (optional)
Tacky glue
Iron and ironing surface

Finished Size: Design area of Santa is 16 stitches wide x 26 stitches high. Reindeer is 18 stitches wide x 21 stitches high. Snowman is 17 stitches wide x 18 stitches high. Completed ornaments are approximately 1-1/4 inches wide x 6 inches tall.

Directions:
STITCHING: Overcast or zigzag edges of Aida cloth to prevent fraying.

To find the center of the cloth, fold it in half lengthwise, then fold in half crosswise and mark this point with water-soluble marker. To find centers of charts, draw lines across charts, connecting arrows. Begin stitching at this point so designs will be centered.

Separate six-strand floss and use two strands for cross-stitching and Eyelet stitching and one strand for back-stitching. (See Fig. 1.)

Each symbol on a chart equals one stitch over a set of fabric threads with different colors representing different colors of floss or stitches. Make stitches in the colors shown on chart or in colors of your choice, first completing all cross-stitching, then backstitching.

Do not knot floss on back of work. Instead, leave a short tail on back and hold in place. Weave tails and ends through stitches as stitching progresses.

When all of the stitching is completed, iron the fusible interfacing onto the back of the stitched design, following the manufacturer's instructions.

Trim, leaving one set of threads beyond the outside of the design. Apply seam sealant to cut edge.

PAINTING: Paint each craft stick according to the painting diagrams on the next page. If necessary, apply more than one coat so color covers craft stick completely. Let dry.

Use black permanent marker to outline legs on Santa and reindeer. Paint red collar and bow on snowman, and green collar and holly on reindeer. Use black marker to add lines to the holly leaves on reindeer. Paint gold buckle on Santa. Dip paintbrush handle in black paint and paint buttons on Santa and snowman. Spray with clear acrylic spray to seal each craft stick.

FINISHING: Glue stitched motifs to top of painted craft sticks. (See craft stick painting diagrams and photo for placement.) Glue pearl cotton thread ends to upper back of craft sticks to create hangers if desired. ❁

Her Plant Pokes Bloom With Christmas Cheer

THANKS TO Renee Dent of Conrad, Montana, your greenery can get decked out for the holidays with pretty plant pokes peeking out! These craft-stick creations also make cute ornaments—just glue a loop of red thread to the back, suggests Renee.

Materials Needed (for all three pokes):
Charts on next page
3-inch square of 14-count white Aida cloth—one per plant poke
DMC six-strand embroidery floss in colors listed on color key or in colors of your choice
3-inch square of fusible interfacing— one per plant poke
Jumbo craft stick—one per plant poke
Acrylic paints—white, black, red, brown, green and metallic gold
Black fine-line permanent marker
Size 24 tapestry needle
Small paintbrush
Scissors
Water-soluble fabric marker
Fray Check or other seam sealant
Clear acrylic craft spray
Three 6-inch lengths of pearl cotton

COLOR KEY

		DMC
⊡	White	
■	Christmas Red Medium	304
■	Black	310
■	Christmas Green Very Dark	699
◢	Salmon Light	761
⊟	Pearl Gray Very Light	762
▨	Peach Flesh Very Light	948
◆	Black/Brown	3371
▦	Rose Brown Dark	3772
☒	Rose Beige	3773

BACKSTITCH

— Black/Brown (one strand) 3371

EYELET STITCH

✳ Salmon Light (two strands) 761

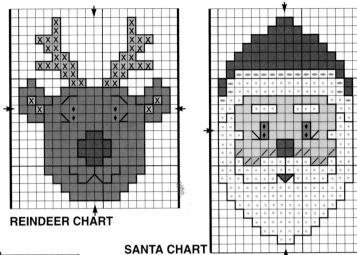

REINDEER CHART

SANTA CHART

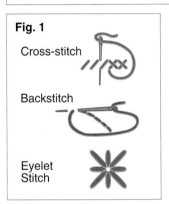

Fig. 1

Cross-stitch

Backstitch

Eyelet
Stitch

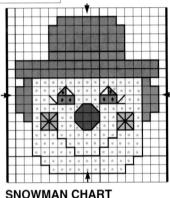

SNOWMAN CHART

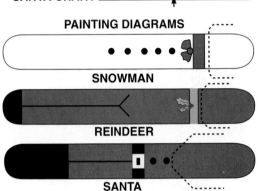

PAINTING DIAGRAMS

SNOWMAN

REINDEER

SANTA

This Place Mat Is in the Cards

HAVE Christmas cards from years past that are just too pretty to throw out? Bring them to dinner instead.

LaRayne Meyer of Pilger, Nebraska uses old holiday greeting cards she's received to quickly create collage place mats. She says doing so is the next best thing to sharing a festive meal with any faraway friends you may have.

Materials Needed:

*11-inch x 16-inch piece
of stiff cardboard
Gold foil gift wrap
Assorted used Christmas
cards
Paper glue
Invisible tape
Scissors
Clear Con-Tact paper or
other adhesive-*

backed protective cover

Finished Size: Place mat is 11 inches x 16 inches.

Directions:

Cut out a 12-1/2-in. x 17-1/2-in. piece of gold foil gift wrap. Cover front of cardboard piece with gift wrap, folding excess to back of cardboard. Miter corners of gift wrap and tape in place on back of cardboard.

Cut out designs from Christmas card fronts, trimming around various shapes and designs on the cards.

Create a collage by arranging shapes on top of gift wrap-covered cardboard. You may use a theme (such as all Santas, Christmas trees or Nativities) or place the shapes randomly. Glue shapes in place.

Cover both sides of the place mat with clear Con-Tact paper. ❧

Stocking Puts Its Best Foot Forward...Front and Back

DOUBLE FUN is afoot with this two-sided stocking! It's perfect for hanging on a staircase or window, where the looking's twice as nice.

Jolly old Santa smiles on one side, while a pretty pine decorates the other. Designer Emma Willey of Winston, Oregon combined two seasonal symbols that make this stocking a treat before the stuffin' even starts!

Materials Needed:
Worsted-weight yarn in 4-ounce skeins—one skein each or leftover amounts of white (A) and black (B), 10 yards of pink (C) and 12 inches of gold (D)

Sport-weight yarn—one skein each or leftover amounts of red (E), white (F) and green (G)

Straight knitting needles—sizes 1 (2.25mm) and 8 (5mm) or sizes needed to obtain correct gauge

Size C/2 (2.75mm) crochet hook

Pom-poms—twelve 1/4-inch red, one each 3/8-inch white and yellow, three 1/2-inch red and one 3/4-inch red

Two 1/4-inch movable eyes

Tapestry needle

Scissors

Polyester stuffing

Straight pins

Tacky (white) glue

Gauge: In St st with worsted-weight yarn and larger size needles, 16 sts and 22 rows = 4 inches. In St st with sport-weight yarn and smaller size needles, 6 sts and 11 rows = 1 inch.

Finished Size: Stocking is about 10 inches long.

Stitches Used:
STOCKINETTE STITCH: St st
   Row 1 (RS): Knit
   Row 2 (WS): Purl
   Repeat Rows 1 and 2.

Directions:
STOCKING: Beginning at top of stocking with larger size needles and A, cast on 41 sts.
   Rows 1-8 (Cuff): Knit.
   Rows 9-30: Work in St st.
   Rows 31-32: Cast on 8 sts at beginning of each row and continue in St st: 57 sts at end of Row 32.

Rows 33-47: Work in St st. Bind off in purl. Fasten off.

CROSS-STITCHING: Each knit stitch counts as one square on the chart, and cross-stitches are stitched with tapestry needle and a single strand of sport-weight yarn in colors shown on color key.

Do not knot yarn on back of work. Instead, leave a short tail on back of work and hold in place. Weave tails and ends through several stitches as stitching progresses.

Making each cross-stitch (Fig. 1) so it covers a single knit stitch, follow chart to stitch HO HO HO HO across top of stocking, beginning upper edge of letters on second stitch below cuff. Follow chart to stitch the Christmas tree, centering it 1-1/4 in. below the two HO HO's stitched on left side of stocking.

SANTA CLAUS SIDE: Use smaller size needles for all Santa pieces.

Boots: With B, cast on 6 sts.

Rows 1-8: Work in St st.

Rows 9-14: With F, knit each row.

Rows 15-20: With E, work in St st. Cut E. Slide work to end of needle.

Repeat Rows 1-20 for second leg, without cutting E at end of Row 20.

Body/Head: Rows 1-6: Working across sts of both legs, continue in St st with E: 12 sts.

Rows 7-8 (Belt): With B, work in St st.

Rows 9-14: With E, work in St st.

Rows 15-16: Bind off 2 sts at beginning of next two rows so 8 sts remain at end of Row 16.

Rows 17-18: Bind off 1 st at beginning of next two rows so 6 sts remain at end of Row 18.

Rows 19-26: With C, work in St st. Bind off.

Arms: With C, cast on 8 sts.

Rows 1-4: Work in St st.

Rows 5-8: With F, knit each row.

Rows 9-14: With E, work in St st. Bind off.

Repeat Rows 1-14 to make a second arm.

Hat: With F, cast on 12 sts.

Rows 1-6: Knit each row.

Row 7: With E, knit.

Row 8: P 2 tog, purl to last 2 sts, p 2 tog.

Rows 9, 11, 13 and 15: With E, sl 1, k 1, psso, k to last 2 sts, k 2 tog: 2 sts remain at end of Row 15.

Rows 10, 12 and 14: Purl.

After Row 15, cut yarn and bring yarn end through remaining 2 sts on needle and fasten off, leaving yarn end for stitching.

Assembly: With F, embroider the hair, mustache and beard using straight stitches and lazy daisy stitches. (See Fig. 1.) Using D, straight-stitch the buckle in the center of the belt.

Fold each arm and boot in half lengthwise, matching ends of rows. Hand-stitch edges together, lightly stuffing each before completely stitching edges together. Stitch only top of arm (red end) to "shoulder" of body, leaving remainder of arm free. Repeat, adding second arm to opposite shoulder.

Fold stocking in half wrong sides together, matching beginning and ends of rows. Pin Santa body/head piece and hat centered on half of stocking as shown in photo. Unfold stocking and use matching yarn to sew Santa body/head onto stocking half, lightly stuffing as piece is stitched on and leaving boots and arms free.

FINISHING: Glue 3/8-in. white pom-pom to tip of Santa's hat and 1/4-in. red pom-pom to his head for nose. Glue eyes in place above nose.

Glue 3/8-in. yellow pom-pom onto top of tree. Glue remaining eleven 1/4-in. red pom-poms randomly onto tree for ornaments.

Fold stocking in half right side out. Use A to stitch front, toe and bottom edges together.

Lastly, glue 3/4-in. red pom-pom onto toe. Glue three 1/2-in. red pom-poms onto front of stocking cuff to resemble holly berries. Let dry.

With C hook and A, chain 27. Fasten off, leaving an 8-in. yarn end. Fold chain in half and use yarn end to stitch both ends of chain to top back edge of stocking for hanging. ❀

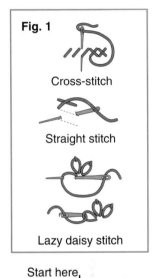

Fig. 1

Cross-stitch

Straight stitch

Lazy daisy stitch

HO HO HO HO CHART

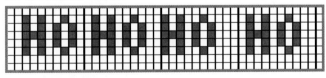

ABBREVIATIONS	
k	knit
p	purl
psso	pass the slipped stitch over
RS	right side
sl	slip
st(s)	stitch(es)
St st	Stockinette stitch
tog	together
WS	wrong side

COLOR KEY
■ Red (E)
▨ Green (G)

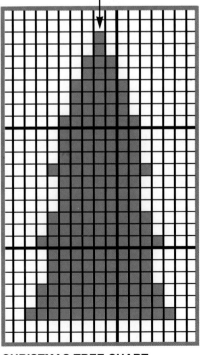

Start here

CHRISTMAS TREE CHART

Cowboy Claus Lassoes Lots of Yuletide Glee

IF you're hopin' to rope an extra dash of down-home feeling for your home on the range, rely on this merry cowpoke. He's decked out in his holiday Western best and ready to round up grins.

All it takes to rustle up a Cowboy Claus is cutting and gluing simple fabric and wood pieces to an egg shape, according to Janna Britton of Firebaugh, California. "He's easy enough for beginners to try," she adds.

Materials Needed:
Patterns on next page
Tracing or pattern paper and pencil
Craft knife
2-1/2-inch plastic, foam or papier-mache egg
1-inch wood ball
One 9-inch x 12-inch piece of red felt
Scrap of antique white plush felt
Satin ribbon—7 inches each of 1/4-inch-wide black and 1/8-inch-wide red
6-1/2-inch-long piece of white curly wool doll hair
3/8-inch pearl snap cover
3-3/4-inch round clothespin or doll pin
Coping or scroll saw
Brown oven-bake polymer clay
Glass baking dish
Powdered blush
Cotton swab

Acrylic craft paints—black, red and white
2-inch red cowboy hat
Fine-liner paintbrush
1-1/2-inch flocked wreath
Two 1/2-inch cowbells
Glue gun and glue sticks or tacky (white) glue
Rotary cutter and mat (optional)
Quilter's ruler (optional)
Scissors
Round toothpick

Finished Size: Cowboy Claus measures about 5 inches high x 3-1/2 inches across.

Directions:
Trace patterns onto tracing or pattern paper. Cut out.

Cut out fabric pieces as indicated on patterns. Also cut one 3-1/2-in.-diameter circle from red felt for pants.

Use rotary cutter and mat or scissors and ruler to cut the following 1/4-in.-wide strips of antique white plush felt: Two 2-in.-long strips for bottom edges of sleeves; one 2-in.-long strip for center front of jacket; one 7-1/2-in.-long strip for bottom edge of jacket; and one 3-in.-long strip for neck edge of jacket.

Use coping or scroll saw to cut clothespin 1-3/4 in. from ends of prongs. Discard top. Prongs will be used for arms.

BOOTS: Soften polymer clay and form two thick rolls. Shape each roll into a cowboy boot, using Boot Illustrations in Fig. 1 as a guide for size and making sure top of each boot fits the curve of the wide end of the egg. Add heels.

Use toothpick to make stitching design on boots as shown in illustration.

Place in glass baking dish and bake, following manufacturer's directions. Let boots cool.

CLOTHING: Center 3-1/2-in. circle of red felt over wide end of egg for pants and glue to egg, smoothing felt evenly over egg.

Glue jacket around top (narrow end) of egg so short edges meet at center front, folding in fullness at top (neck) edge of jacket.

Glue one sleeve around one clothespin prong with long edges on inside of prong, leaving about 1/4 in. of prong end showing for hand. Wrap top of sleeve over cut end of clothespin. Trim as needed. Repeat for second arm.

Glue plush felt strips around bottom edge of jacket, over center front edges of jacket, around neck edge of jacket and around bottom edges of sleeves just above hands, as shown in photo above left. Trim as needed.

Glue black ribbon around jacket 1/4 in. above plush felt strip, overlapping at center front.

Glue snap cover over black ribbon at center front.

Glue arms to sides of egg about 1 in. from center top of egg, angling arms toward front.

HEAD/FACE: Glue wood ball to top of egg/jacket.

Using fine-liner brush and referring to painting diagram, paint two small black dots for eyes on front of wood ball. Let dry. Paint a tiny red dash for nose. Let dry. Paint tiny white highlight in each eye. Let dry.

Place a small amount of powdered blush on cotton swab and add to cheek area, using a circular motion.

BEARD AND HAIR: Cut 2-1/2 in. of wool hair and fold in half lengthwise, spreading slightly. Glue fold to head just under nose from cheek to cheek. Fluff beard.

Cut two 2-in. lengths of wool hair and glue one length from side to side across top of head. Glue other length from front to back over top of head to form bangs and hair down back of head to the edge of the jacket.

FINISHING: Stand boots up on flat surface. Set bottom of Cowboy Claus body on top of boots. When body is centered and balances on top of boots, glue boots to body.

Glue cowboy hat onto top of head.

Thread red ribbon through tops of two cowbells and wrap ribbon around wreath. Tie ends of ribbon into a 1-in. bow at front of wreath. Trim ends as desired. Glue wreath to Cowboy Claus' right hand, as shown in photo. ❄

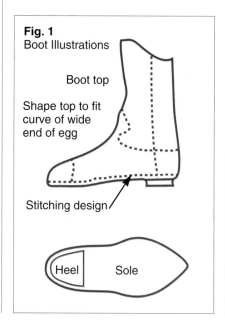

Fig. 1
Boot Illustrations

Boot top

Shape top to fit curve of wide end of egg

Stitching design

Heel   Sole

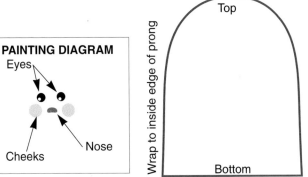

PAINTING DIAGRAM

Eyes

Cheeks

Nose

SLEEVE PATTERN
Cut 2—red felt

Wrap to inside edge of prong

Top

Bottom

JACKET PATTERN
Cut 1—red felt

Fold in fullness

Neck edge

Place on fold

Center front

Bottom

Tuck Away Tissues—in a Crafty Ho-Ho-Holder

WITH this handy holiday holder, you can keep tissues at your fingertips *and* in Yuletide style.

Linda Whitener of Glen Allen, Missouri came up with the pretty yet practical container sized right for a packet of tissues. Her easy-to-stitch idea looks nice on the kitchen counter, plus it tucks tidily into your purse.

Materials Needed (for one holder):
Fabric for holder—two 1-1/4-inch x 6-inch pieces of Christmas print or plain solid for inside top edge, two 1-1/2-inch x 6-inch pieces of coordinating print or plaid for outside top edge and one 4-inch x 6-inch piece for bottom to coordinate with top fabrics*

Fabric for lining—two 2-1/4-inch x 6-inch pieces of white solid for top and one 4-inch x 6-inch piece of white solid for bottom

Quilt batting—two 2-1/4-inch x 6-inch pieces for top and one 4-inch x 6-inch piece for bottom

All-purpose sewing thread in matching or contrasting colors
Scissors
Standard sewing supplies
Iron and ironing surface
*Linda used a large green Christmas print for the inside top edges and bottom, and a small green Christmas print for the outside top edges of one holder. For the other, she used red plaid for the outside top edges and bottom, and blue chambray for the inside top edges.

Finished Size: Tissue holder measures 5-1/2 inches x 3-1/2 inches.

Directions: Machine-wash, dry and press all fabrics. Use 1/4-in. seams with right sides of fabric together unless otherwise directed.

TOP: Pin one long edge of one inside top piece and one long edge of one outside top piece together and machine-stitch. Press the seam open. Repeat with the remaining inside and outside top pieces.

Place one top lining piece on top of one joined top piece on flat surface. Place one top batting piece on top and pin all three layers together. Machine-stitch along inside top edge of pinned pieces. Remove pins. Open and turn lining and batting to wrong side. Hand-baste all layers together, matching raw edges. Topstitch along seam edge. Machine-quilt top as desired. Zigzag-stitch around the three open edges. Remove basting. Repeat with other top, lining and batting pieces.

Place seamed edges of top pieces together so they are just touching but not overlapping. Stitch edges together using wide zigzag stitch through each seam edge, as shown in Fig. 1. Set aside.

BACK: Place bottom lining right side down on flat surface. Place bottom batting on top of lining and bottom backing fabric right side up on top of batting. Hand-baste through all layers, matching all raw edges. Machine-quilt layers together as desired. Zigzag around all

edges. Remove basting.

FINISHING: Place top and bottom of holder right sides together, matching outside edges and pin in place. Machine-stitch around outside edges. Trim seams and clip corners. Turn right side out through top opening.

Insert a small packet of tissues through opening. ❀

Fig. 1
Holder top

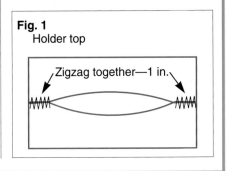

Zigzag together—1 in.

OUT OF THE WOODS, Becky Stegenga (bottom) creatively coaxes holiday custom of Yule log.

At Christmastime, Crafter Creates a Colorful Logjam

HAPPY HOLIDAYS grow on trees—at least they do around Becky Stegenga's woodsy cottage in the small town of Portland, Michigan.

"My favorite Christmas project is making decorative Yule logs," relates the creative wife and mother.

"I began 4 years ago, fashioning them for family and friends. Then people started asking if they could buy them. So I launched a sideline to finance my Christmas present fund."

Becky credits two sources for her inspiration—"Father Christmas *and* Mother Nature, who provides most of my crafting material. Every autumn, my husband, Mike, our 11-year-old, Laura, and I help thin surplus trees from a relative's woods and put our harvest to good use as Yule logs.

"I look for a soft maple with smooth bark and straight branches. Mike cuts it into logs for me. We even salvage the stump. It makes a perfect centerpiece."

The week before Thanksgiving, the logs are brought out of storage and brushed clean before Becky gets going rolling out her fresh-from-the-forest decor. "I cover the top with melted wax," she informs.

"Often, I use green candle wax with a spicy bayberry scent, in keeping with the essence of the season. I just pretend I'm 'frosting' the log…like Christmas cookies.

"While the wax is still sticky, I affix pinecones and sprigs of evergreen that Laura and I have collected. Next, I add homegrown dried-flower accents and spray-on glitter and snow for a dusting of holiday magic.

"As a finishing touch, I add a tag explaining the Old World roots of the Yule log. Years ago on Christmas Eve, it was brought in, garlanded with greens and lit with great celebration. The charred remnants were saved and used during the New Year to protect the household, remedy illness and enrich the harvest."

Today, Becky's logs more often warm hearts as the nostalgic focus of tables, mantels and hearths. "Many customers come back year after year," she gladly reports. "It's nice to know I've had a part in helping start some new old-fashioned family traditions."

Pining for a Yule Log?

BECAUSE THEY'RE so fragile, Becky can't ship her arrangements by mail. But she's happy to tell you how to make your own Yule log:

• Begin with a soft wood log such as maple or birch, 5 inches in diameter and cut to a length of 1 foot.

• Remove any residue.

• Make sure the log is dry and at room temperature.

• Melt candle wax (with a Christmasy scent and color if you wish) in a double boiler at a low temperature, taking care not to leave it unattended. (Thrifty hint: Have stubs of used candles around? Melt them.)

• When wax is melted, pour it into an old tin container for easy access. Using a spatula or putty knife, apply a base coat of wax to the top of the log.

• Push pinecones and other heavy accents into the wax first—placing them on their base or side.

• Attach sprigs of evergreens so that needles fan out on all sides of the log along its top.

• If the wax is hardening and losing its tackiness, drizzle on more melted wax between the attached items. A glue gun works well for emergency repairs, too.

• Add dried accents (such as yarrow, statice, rose hips, thistles) and small beads, mini ornaments and chestnuts if desired.

• Drizzle a little more melted wax over the pinecones, letting it trickle down and harden on the sides of the log.

• Spray crafter's glitter over the top. Then "frost" the tips of the greens with spray-on snow.

• As a festive finishing touch, tie a big bow in a bright holiday hue around your Yule log. ❀

Readers' Poetry Corner

Christmas Memories

Softly falls the winter darkness,
While I sit beside this tree—
Decked with ornaments of silver,
Trimmed with precious memories.

Lumpy wreaths of salt and flour,
Clothespin reindeer, wiggly-eyed;
Crocheted snowflakes, baby angels,
Golden horns with ribbons tied.

Tiny lights of blue and scarlet
Sparkling in the festive room;
Standing tall, the stately pine tree
Fills the air with its perfume.

All too soon, I'll turn the lights off,
Put the ornaments away,
Wrap the angel up in tissue
For another Christmas Day.

So I sit here in the darkness,
With my dreams of Christmas past,
Lost in quiet reminiscence…
For the years go by so fast.

—**Dawn E. McCormick**
Spring, Texas

Homemade for the Holidays Are Cards

The fun way some families put their stamp on the season could cause even Scrooge to smile. Here's the happy picture proof...

REJOICE!

A SAVIOR IS BORN

LITTLEST ANGEL Kaitlin Elizabeth Milligan earned her wings by gracing her family's heaven-sent Christmas card. Don't let those wide innocent eyes fool you, advises Mom Joy from Indianola, Iowa: "Our angel is a normal, typically curious tyke, full of spirit year-round."

Happy Holidays

Peace on Earth

WE WADED A LONG TIME TO FIND EACH OTHER. NOW WE ARE ENGAGED!

Bruce and Sheila

THREE CHEERS are delivered by the Liette brothers of Sidney, Ohio—left to right, Jordon, Josh and Michael. "The boys all enjoy modeling holiday outfits," writes their mother, Angela. "My husband, Duaine, and I treasure each one of the fun annual snapshots we use as our Christmas cards."

MARRY CHRISTMAS. An engaging image did double duty as a season's greeting and a wedding announcement, explains Sheila Flodin of Farmington, Minnesota. "The photo shows the love Bruce and I have for fishing and each other," she notes of how she and he chose to ring in the New Year.

JINGLE BULLS? Chuckles by the mailboxful could be "herd" from the recipients of Mardell and Dennis Kirchhoff's leg-pulling greeting. "It was trick photography that placed our 'sitting bull' on the sled," Mardell 'fesses up from Tripoli, Iowa.

US TO YULE. "This postcard let us welcome loved ones across the nation to our Amish country home for the holidays," relates Julia Horst of Gordonville, Pennsylvania on behalf of husband Jeff plus Melissa, Tanner, Hamilton and Marshall.

 PEACE ON EARTH

PRECIOUS MOMENT of the first Nativity is sweetly revisited by her great-grandchildren—Destenee, Landry and baby Heidi—on their family's greeting, jots Mary June Hardy of Walsh, Colorado. "Their handy dad built the scene," she adds.

UNDER THEIR CAPS, Christie and Michael Phillips look a little different than they do today. "Although they're both in college now, I thought it would be fun to reuse this favorite Christmas card," says their mother, Debbie, of Farwell, Texas. "It reflects our annual tradition of giving them new pj's to wear on Christmas Eve."

WISHING YOU A WONDERFUL CHRISTMAS And a Happy New Year!

YAPPY HOLIDAYS. Nancy Thackston's "grandpuppies" make cute-as-can-be photo subjects, this fetchingly festive message attests. "I regularly take 'the boys' to visit folks at the local nursing home for some furry TLC," she reports from Hiram, Georgia about doggone adorable quartet.

Four Loving Hands Led the Way to Christmas

By Trudy Duivenvoorden Mitic of Victoria, British Columbia

inter always arrived early on our northern-New Brunswick dairy farm when I was growing up. But it was no match for a pair of parents determined to make their children's Christmas happy.

Each day, the horse-drawn sled would carry cans of still-warm milk to the highway, where Dad's truck was waiting. Later, it would return with empty cans—plus an assortment of supplies from the nearby village and the day's mail.

The day the sled's bounty included the Simpson-Sears Christmas catalog, we knew the season was officially under way. While our parents deliberated how to make ends meet, we savored the glossy pages. Never once did we doubt that the most special of holidays would be joyous at our house.

During those long December nights, we were coaxed into bed extra early. With a hot water bottle at my feet and an old sheepskin jacket tucked around my shoulders, I would fall asleep to the moan of the wind outside and the soothing mechanical whir of my mother's sewing machine downstairs.

Plenty to Do

If mending was a nightly routine for her, my father's days were long and arduous, too.

When the thermometer plunged below zero, water bowls froze and the barn cleaner became undependable. In his "spare" time, Dad shoveled snow and chopped wood for the ever-hungry farmhouse furnace.

Through it all, Christmas crept closer. Still, the winter rhythms of the farm prevailed.

For us children, there were mangers to be swept (although it was easy to become distracted by the intricately patterned hoarfrost on the single-paned barn windows). There was hay to toss down from the ice-cold loft (but dustings of sparkling snow on the barn rafters begged to be swept up on bulky woolen mittens and sampled).

Back in the warmth of the barn, we forked bits of straw under the calves and pondered aloud the possibility that they might somehow know more about the mir-

acle of this very special season than we did.

Finally, Christmas came. We struggled home from church through the snow. Then, with great expectation, we gathered around the tinseled homegrown tree.

There was no money for wrapping paper, of course. So the treasures lay concealed under a large white bed sheet. When all was ready, Mom—her eyes sparkling—pulled the sheet away to reveal a magical collection of surprises.

Surrounded by Love

The year I was 8, my gift was a store-bought doll with blue eyes and blonde curls. She was delicately beautiful, exuding a wonderful scent of pink-plastic newness.

Decades later, however, what I remember most are the things that came with her.

My doll was nestled in a pink crib—crafted by Dad out of a lowly orange crate. Mom had meticulously made a mattress to fit, a miniature quilt, a lace-edged sheet and pillow, and clothes including striped pajamas.

My 7-year-old sister's gift was much the same. One of the younger children received a tricycle, lovingly restored and gleaming with fresh paint.

Looking back, I marvel at my parents' perseverance. Many nights, after we youngsters had been tucked into bed, they worked together past midnight at the kitchen table.

Team with Spirit

Mom sat at her designated spot, a tabletop sewing machine in front of her and a box of fabric scraps at her elbow. Dad was across the table, sanding or painting one of his painstaking projects. The ache of work-weary muscles temporarily forgotten, they enjoyed coffee and easy conversation as they planned and created each gift.

The doll I received that year is long gone. But I still have the crib, bedding and homemade doll clothes.

When the holiday glitz of today threatens to overwhelm me, I turn to those cherished possessions. They remind me of the essence of Christmas—that the greatest gifts, the most wondrous offerings, carry no price tag…they spring instead from a loving heart. ❈

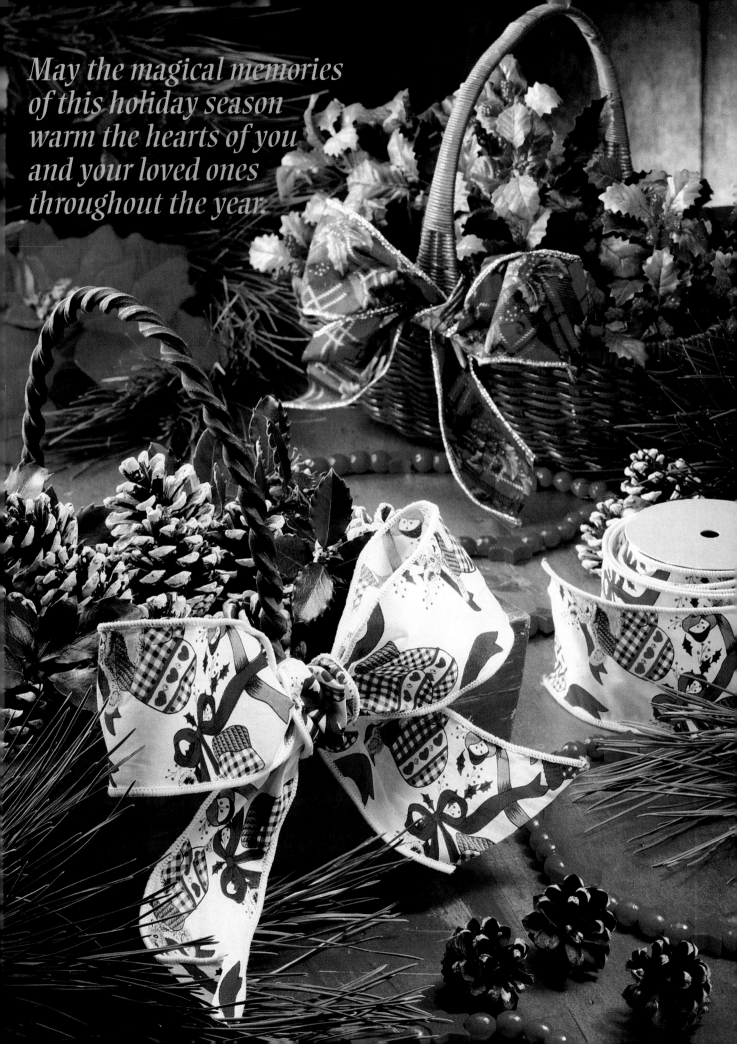

*May the magical memories
of this holiday season
warm the hearts of you
and your loved ones
throughout the year.*

INDEX

Share Your Holiday Joy with Others...

DO *YOU* celebrate Christmas in a special way? If so, we'd like to know! We're already gathering material for our next *Country Woman Christmas* book. And we need your help!

Do you have a nostalgic holiday-related story to share? Perhaps you have penned a Christmas poem...or a heartwarming fiction story?

Does your family carry on a favorite holiday tradition? Or do you deck your halls in a festive way? Maybe you've started a Christmas-related enterprise...or know of a Christmas-loving country woman others might like to meet?

We're looking for *original* Christmas quilt patterns and craft projects, too, plus homemade Nativities, gingerbread houses, etc. Don't forget to include your best recipes for holiday-favorite main-dish meats, home-baked cookies, candies, breads, etc.!

Send your ideas and photos to "*CW* Christmas Book", 5925 Country Lane, Greendale WI 53129. (Enclose a self-addressed stamped envelope if you'd like materials returned.)